Hannah Cornaby

Autobiography and Poems

Hannah Cornaby

Autobiography and Poems

ISBN/EAN: 9783744713511

Printed in Europe, USA, Canada, Australia, Japan

Cover: Foto ©Thomas Meinert / pixelio.de

More available books at **www.hansebooks.com**

Autobiography and Poems
by Hannah Cornaby.

*The prayer is breathed, that on each path
Truth's own pure light may shine,
Brightening the sombre hues of earth
With radiance divine.
Onward and upward, clear and bright,
May it direct our course
Back to the fountain head of light,
Its own eternal source.*

SALT LAKE CITY:
PRINTED BY J. C. GRAHAM & CO.
1881.

PREFACE.

IN introducing this little work to the public, hope and fear alternately plead for supremacy; in vain I try to still the tumult; the desire to merit the approbation of my readers is naturally uppermost; hence comes the fear of not attaining the object which has induced me to lay aside the doubts that have long prevented my attempt to gather up some of the fragments, which at sundry times, and under various circumstances have been written; and very humbly do I ask that the reader may exercise that "fervent charity," beneath whose broad mantle my many imperfections, I trust, may be covered.

Most reluctantly have I entered upon the work; long and severe has been the struggle between my natural timidity and reserve, and the fear of incurring the displeasure of my Father in Heaven, by failing to observe the injunction of Paul to Timothy: "Neglect not the gift that is in thee, which was given thee by prophecy."

Weighed down by the sense of accountability, and the consciousness of my inability to attain the standard of excellence necessary to enable me to soar above the shafts of criticism, my mind has suffered from misgivings; especially when standing, apparently in the presence of death, has a sense of my ingratitude, in not having placed in a position to live, some of the most important events of my life, almost overwhelmed me.

The ability to write, which at first seemed given only to while away the hours of sickness, I found, to my great joy, enabled me also, to encourage and comfort others. Some of my pieces were written when life was, to all human appearance, fast ebbing out; hence the earnestness which characterizes them. Confined for years to the sick room, I seemingly lived in the presence of the searcher of hearts; and with the consciousness, "Thou, God, seest me," I dare only write *truthfully*; and feeble as I was, when an inspiration was felt, I endeavored to commit it to paper in the simplest manner, unadorned by the flowers of rhetoric.

A number of my pieces have been written at the request of friends, and are thus of a personal character, which some may consider objectionable; but the motive prompting them has induced their insertion, as they may contain some sentiment that may help others than those for whom they were originally penned.

The insertion of names may be subject to censure; for which I trust to be pardoned, as in most instances they are but grateful reminders of kindly deeds, for " The righteous shall be had in everlasting remembrance." In this connection, I cannot omit to mention the kind encouragement and able assistance rendered by Bishop Charles D. Evans of Salem, in revising my manuscript for the press.

I have endeavored to narrate, in simple and unadorned language, the experience of one whose highest ambition is to be a faithful Latter-day Saint, and to tell the peace and joy which a knowledge of the Gospel has brought to one of its humble followers ; and if its perusal should cause any, unacquainted with the religion of Jesus Christ, to seek to know if these things are so ; or if my experience should lead some drooping one to take fresh courage ; or be a source of pleasure ; if the young should learn from it, that "Wisdom's ways are pleasant, its paths peace," and should be induced to walk therein, I shall feel amply rewarded ; although

      I scarcely dare to think that God
        Would give to one so small,
      Aught that could cheer another on,
        Or help His cause at all.
      But oh! I prize above all else,
        The power to chase away
      Sorrow or pain from those I meet
        While trav'ling life's highway.

THE AUTHOR.

CONTENTS.

AUTOBIOGRAPHY.

	Page
Chapter I.—Early Influences	9
Chapter II.—Love and Wedlock	15
Chapter III.—The Light of the Gospel	21
Chapter IV.—My Native Land, Farewell	29
Chapter V.—Manna in the Wilderness	36
Chapter VI.—Pioneer Difficulties	43
Chapter VII.—Miraculous Healing	51
Chapter VIII.—Conclusion	59

POEMS.

	Page
Crossing the Atlantic Ocean	65
A Similitude	84
Contemplations	85
Who's on the Lord's side	88
Christmas in my Childhood's Home	90
To a Tulip	93
Woman's Mission	94
"Another Outrage."	95
A True Story	96
Co-operation	97
To Bishop Albert K. Thurber	99
Our Native Flowers	101
To the Relief Society of Spanish Fork	102
Comments on Acts, 3rd Chapter, 6th verse	104
Utah	105

CONTENTS.

	Page		Page
To Mrs.———	106	Beautiful Mountain Home	133
The Two Deacons	108	To Mrs. Mary Isaacs	134
A Fragment	109	Lead Me to the Rock	135
Provo Woolen Factory	110	Winter	136
Invocation	112	July 24th, 1872	137
"I was Sick, and ye visited me."	114	Musings	138
		Song—Deseret	139
Jubilee Hymn	116	Truth	140
Autumn	118	Welcome	141
To My Husband	119	Song—Strive for the Right	143
When I'm Happy	121	Consolation	144
To Elder Geo. W. Wilkins	122	Returning Missionaries	145
Pioneer Day	123	Memory of Childhood	146
Mutability	125	December 25th	148
Re-Union of the Y. L. M. I. A.	125	Departing Missionaries	150
		A Song of Praise	152
We are Marching On	127	A Happy New Year	153
To Mrs. S. M. Heywood	128	Think of Thy Mother	155
A Plea for the Relief Society	129	On the Birth of our Grandson	156
A Prayer	131		
To Mrs. Mary Ann Jones	132	Response to Mrs. R———	157

AUTOBIOGRAPHY

CHAPTER I.

EARLY INFLUENCES.

SURELY "goodness and mercy have followed me all the days of my life," I am compelled to acknowledge, as from the grave of the buried past, I seek to bring forth some events in my life, which, for the glory of God, and the good of my fellow creatures, ought not to be lost in oblivion. I realize that if I have received but one talent, I am accountable to the Giver for the proper use of the same; which consideration has induced me to write a short history of my life, in order that my verses may be better understood.

I am the eldest child of William Last and Hannah Hollingsworth. My father was the eldest son of James Last, and Eve Woods; my mother, the youngest child of Samuel Hollingsworth and Lydia Goddard, of the parish of Hoten, near the town of Halesworth, county of Suffolk, England. I was born March 17th, 1822, in Rose Hall, an ancient mansion, situated on the banks of the river Waveny, near Beccles, Suffolk, England. My parents were members of the Episcopal, or Established Church, and honored their profession by serving God, according to the light they possessed.

I was early taught by them to love that Being, who has made the earth so beautiful, and provided so much for His creatures dwelling thereon; thus I was early led to admire and reverence the Creator through His works; and especially from my mother's teaching, learned my duty to Him, as revealed in the Bible. This sacred book was my mother's companion by day and by night; and before able to read, I had committed to memory, under her tuition, many of its holy precepts. When, at six years of age, I began to trace the simpler portions myself, I knew no greater enjoyment than reading its pages, and I committed to memory much of the New Testament and the Psalms.

I was much alone in my early childhood, my brother and sister, Benjamin and Eliza, who were twins, having died at an early age; and my sister Lydia, though I loved her tenderly, was too young for a companion; but to this sweet child,—who for a few years gladdened our home, then went back to her home above, to which, even while on earth she seemed to belong,—I shall have occasion to again refer.

While I was yet too young to appreciate the picturesque beauty of my childhood's home, reverses came to our family, and Rose Hall was exchanged for a suburban cottage, a short distance from our former residence; and here, surrounded by rural scenery, and a pleasant cottage garden, the first remembered events of my life transpired.

When I was about seven years of age, the most wonderful and venerated event of my life occurred, although I cannot recollect the exact date thereof. I have never written an account of this circumstance, realizing that no language of mine could adequately describe it; and now, after a period of fifty years, a feeling of awe comes over me, which I try in vain to overcome.

My father and I were walking in our garden one evening, in the mellow twilight, and a quiet gray beauty pervaded the scene, when a sudden flash of light made us start; and turning towards the point whence it proceeded, we saw a remarkable streak of red, rising in the west, which riveted our attention by its brightness. While watching its upward course, an arm, and a hand holding a roll were plainly visible; and soon the form of a person appeared, full in sight, following the streak of red before mentioned; a light, similar to the first, followed this wonderful personage, and the whole procession slowly moved through the midst of the heavens, and disappeared at the eastern boundary of the horizon. During the passage of this heavenly being across the entire arch of the sky, the right hand was in motion, waving the roll, as if showing it to the inhabitants of the earth. This wonderful vision having disappeared, my father and I, hand in hand, stood as if spell bound, when we heard two men passing along the road, (from which a living fence or hedge separated us,) discoursing on what they, as well as ourselves, had seen. The one remarked to the other, that he thought it could not be an angel, as no wings were visible; we, too, had observed this, yet believed it to be an angel. A loose robe covered the body, leaving the arms and a portion of the limbs visible.

As soon as we were able to walk, we went to the house, when mother saw that something unusual had happened, and asked what made us so pale. At my request, father allowed me to relate to her what we had seen. When I had given an account of this strange phenomenon, she was much affected, and remarked that it was one of the signs of the last days, which, according to the Revelations of St. John, would transpire.

I had loved God before; now I feared and reverenced Him; and desired to know more of that Being who rules in the heavens above, and on the earth beneath. I loved to be alone, especially at eventide, to watch the heavens, thinking another angel would appear; by degrees, however, this desire to watch, wore off. I was attending school, and my lessons, requiring attention, diverted my mind.

About this time I had a companion of my own age, an orphan girl, named Maria Springer, who came to live with her grandfather, Robert Sharman, overseer of a brick-yard and pottery, near our home. We attended the same school, and our play hours being spent together, her presence was a great comfort to me.

I delighted in reading, my parents providing books suited to my age, and was very much interested in a monthly periodical, called the *Child's Companion*, first published in 1830, by the Religious Tract Society.

Ours was a happy fireside ; my maternal grandmother lived with us, on an annuity of her own, and contributed much to the comfort of the family; the children thus receiving many little indulgences not otherwise attainable.

As the years passed on, there seems nothing to record, except that my religious desires deepened and my anxiety to understand the plan of human redemption increased. I attended public worship with my parents, who began to be dissatisfied with the religious tenets they had espoused. My mother was the first to dissent. Attracted by the earnest eloquence of the Rev. Thomas Morell, a Congregationalist minister, she became a member of that denomination, with which she remained satisfied until her death.

Soon a deep sorrow invaded our home ; my sister Lydia sickened, and no mortal power could stay the hand of the destroyer, Death. She had been the light and joy of our hearts and home for eleven years; and her death caused a void that never could be filled. I was fourteen years old when this great trouble came to us. We had been tenderly attached to each other, shared the same room and bed, knelt side by side, morning and evening, to pray, when her pleadings with the Father of her spirit were the most earnest I ever heard. He answered her prayer, and taught her by His holy spirit, how original sin was atoned for in the death of Jesus Christ. I remember her tears of joy on telling us this; and her opening the little Testament and reading to us the 9th and 10th Chaps. of Hebrews, as the foundation of her hopes. She took leave of each of us most affectionately, and gave to each, tokens of remembrance. She passed away peacefully, August 7th, 1836. My two little sisters, Amelia and Mary Ann, were too young to fully understand the loss of this beloved sister; but I mourned so deeply that my health became impaired. Our family physician prescribing change of air and scene, my alarmed parents decided to act upon his advice; meanwhile I was praying to God for help to control my grief, desiring again to see my beloved sister; and this desire was granted me.

One Sunday afternoon, feeling too unwell to go to church, I remained at home, the other members of the family attending. Thus alone, my thoughts reverted to my sister; when lo! she stood before me, as when in perfect health and loveliness. My first impulse was to embrace her, but she moved from me, saying, "No, dear, you cannot." I was disappointed at this, and tried again to clasp her in my arms; but she again assured me I could not, and I had to be content to talk to her at a distance. I asked her if she lived in Heaven; she replied, "I am where Jesus is, will that satisfy you?" I said, "Yes;" and asked how her clothes had been kept so well; she replied, "You remember, that while the children of Israel traveled in the wilderness, their clothes did not wax old; mine are preserved on the same principle." After some further conversation, she disappeared, keeping her face towards me until she vanished from sight. During her stay, and after she left, I was not in the least alarmed. I knew she had come from the spirit world to gratify my longing desire to see her. On their return, I told my parents what had happened and they thought it was a dream, but I knew I was awake at the time, although, at my mother's request, I afterwards told it as a dream.

From this time my mind was satisfied, and my interest in life returned: but my health continued to fail, and my parents were studying how to procure for me the desired change, when a lady of our acquaintance, returning from abroad to her home in Clapham, London, wrote inviting me to stay with her. We thought this very providential, and preparations were made for my immediate departure; but I did not feel as if all was right; I had a dread of London, and the snares and temptations set for the young there. On the day preceding that fixed for my journey, I was very unhappy. The thought of leaving my home and its associations was more painful than can be described. I looked at the traveling trunks, packed by my tender mother's careful hand, and wept bitterly, until my overcharged heart was relieved. Taking Bible in hand I went to my room, and locked the door. Opening the sacred book at the words of Moses, "If Thy presence go not with us, carry us not up hence," I knelt, and taking those words for my prayer, repeated them until the answer came in the words found in Hosea, 2nd Chap. 6th verse, "I will hedge up thy way with thorns." I pondered long on the meaning of the words; and feeling that the intended journey would not be for my good, I decided not to take it.

My parents, though surprised at this decision, acquiesced when I told them of my conviction. My fare, which had been paid to London by stage, we had to lose. Afterwards, we were satisfied that an overruling hand had directed this, as it had many other affairs of my life, for good.

A few days after this, and while we were planning a visit to my aunt Royal, who lived in the city of Norwich, a gentleman who lived near us, called to ask if mother could spare me for a short time, as his children, just deprived by death of their mother, had promised, that if I would stay with them, they would not grieve. My mother consented on condition that my health should be carefully studied, and my education continued; and extracted from me a promise that I would not read works of fiction, as she considered them exceedingly pernicious to the young. This promise I faithfully kept, devoting my leisure hours to reading works of biography, travels, history and theology; which, young as I was, my mind, enlightened by the spirit which giveth light, in a measure comprehended.

CHAPTER II.

LOVE AND WEDLOCK.

MY new home was all that could be desired. The sweet motherless children were prepared to love me; and I, with an aching heart for the loss of my sister, gladly returned their love. They had been well trained by their departed mother; and to instruct them was an easy task. We daily rambled in the fields and meadows which surrounded our pleasant home. Under these favorable influences, my health quickly improved; and as the days and weeks sped on, I scarcely noted time's rapid flight; until many months had passed when Mr.——

brought home a wife to fill the vacant place. My thoughts then turned to the home I still loved so dearly; but it was decided that I could not yet be spared; and my parents, by this time accustomed to my absence, allowed me to remain.

I could fill a volume, describing the admirable qualities of this accomplished lady; but my limited space will only admit a brief notice; too brief, indeed, to do justice to her memory. Perhaps, in the spirit world, to which she has gone, she knows of, and appreciates this humble tribute. Her influence was soon felt by every member of the household. She was benevolent, and had a large visiting district, and none within its limits suffered for anything she had the power to bestow. By degrees, as her domestic duties increased, this part fell to my share; and with my desire to do good, became a very pleasing duty.

One bond of union in this family was the meeting of all its members, morning and evening, for family worship; parents, children, servants and visitors, all met on common ground, to worship God. When all were seated, every one, from the oldest to the youngest, repeated a portion of scripture; one verse at least, giving Book, Chapter and verse. The head of the family then read a chapter in the Bible, which was followed by prayer; when all separated to attend to their respective duties.

During the six years' residence in this family, I had the privilege of attending religious meetings, Bible classes, lectures, &c. On the 4th day of June, in the year 1841, I was publicly received as a member of the Congregational Church, under the pastoral care of the Rev. John Flower.

I can hardly estimate the value of the mental and moral culture I received during this part of my life. My mind expanded like an opening flower to the glad sunshine; but I did not live to myself. I saw misery, want and suffering around me, and in every way in my power, tried to alleviate it. I became deeply interested in Foreign missions, through listening to the eloquent appeals of Williams, Moffat, Pritchard, and other distinguished missionaries; I also labored for the emancipation of the slaves in the West Indies and was present at the meeting held at the hour in which the fetters of slavery were broken, and three millions of human beings, hitherto held in galling chains, set free. My heart still bled for the slaves in America, that land of boasted liberty, and my indignation was raised to burning shame, as, occasionally, an escaped slave reached our land of freedom, and told of the sufferings of his fellows in slavery.

I knew, from the Bible, that God had made of one blood, all who dwell on the face of the earth. I brooded over the negro's wrongs, until I hated the land where laws existed, making one man the property of another, never dreaming that from *that land*, would come to me a deliverance from stronger fetters than those by which the negro slaves were bound,— even deliverance from sectarian dogmas, to the light of the Gospel. Up to this time, I had not even heard that the Gospel had been restored by the hand of an angel, to Joseph Smith, the Prophet of this dispensation.

I find it difficult to cull from the history of my life during this period; each part was real and earnest, and each day found me actively employed.

"Suitors came, my hand to claim," but as yet, my heart gave no response to the symphony of love; though appreciating the honor they sought to confer on me. My friends blamed, and predicted for me the fate of an old maid; this, however, did not distress me; my Bible said, "be not unequally yoked with unbelievers," and thinking myself a believer, feared to be yoked with an unbeliever; none of those who had presented themselves making any profession of religion.

But a day came, when, as in all my life, I had been "led in a way I knew not;" so, with this important step it was the same.

One day I was in the town on business, walking along Market Street, intent only on the errand which called me there, when I met a young man, an entire stranger to me. Now this was nothing remarkable in a busy town like Beccles, nor was there anything remarkable in the appearance of this stranger; but something whispered, "That is your future husband." Surprised at this, I turned to take a look at him, and, to my annoyance, he had also turned to look at me. Ashamed of myself for this breach of street etiquette, I hastily resumed my way, and this stranger, who had thus attracted my attention was lost to sight. Not so with the interest he had created in my heart. Business was for the time forgotten; I walked aimlessly on, thinking of this strange event, when I was met by my sister Amelia, who asked what had happened to make me look so pleased. I told her frankly of the singular circumstance just recorded. She smiled, and said, "Oh, my romantic sister." I replied, "Do not make fun of me; I shall marry that man, or I shall never marry on this earth." I told other of my friends the same. I had never seen this man before; I might never see him again; but this made no difference. I spent hours, "dreaming love's first dream," happy in thinking, that sometime, either in this probation or another, I should meet him again.

Months rolled on; another element had come into my existence. I could not drive from my thoughts this singular incident, when, apparently by the merest accident, at the house of a friend, I met, and was introduced to Mr. Cornaby, who had come to Beccles to take charge of a public school; and here, dear reader, let me introduce to you my future husband; for in this gentleman I recognized the mysterious stranger, who for months had filled my thoughts. Though perturbed and agitated, I concealed my emotion, and left the house as quickly as possible; and in the quietude of my own room, thought and prayed earnestly for the guidance of the holy spirit to direct me aright. Accidental meetings with Mr. Cornaby frequently happened after this. Our acquaintance ripened into friendship; and a sympathy, which neither of us understood, was making that friendship a necessity.

Three delightful years followed; but a description of those years, though pleasing to me, would not interest my readers. Up to this time, love had never been mentioned; and Mr. Cornaby knew nothing of the sentiment that was filling my life. He had ambitious aspirations for his future; and often spoke of leaving Beccles to enter a college in London. In pursuance of this plan, the time came for our adieus to be said, and he took his departure to London for an indefinite period while I was left to pursue "the even tenor of my way,"—to seek for strength to bear this trial of my faith and, as usual, to draw comfort and satisfaction from the assurance, that "all things work together for good to those who love God." I resumed my somewhat neglected duties, becoming more assiduous in my visits to the sick and needy, reading to them, and schooling myself into the belief that I was meeting the reward I merited, in allowing myself to set up an idol in my heart.

We corresponded frequently, and the letters from London were always welcome; but at length ceased, and weeks of suspense ensued. I then learned that the object of my solicitude lay dangerously sick of lung fever; but after days of anxious waiting, a letter from himself, written in a trembling hand, told that the doctor pronounced him out of danger, but advised removal to his native air. At the time this intelligence reached me, I was watching beside the sick bed of a friend, whom I could not leave until the danger was passed; by which time, Mr. Cornaby had been removed to Lowestoft,—his native town,—and breathing the bracing sea air, was returning to health.

During the weeks of convalescence which followed, he visited Beccles; and it was then, while rambling together along the delicious green lanes for which England is so famed, in that loveliest of all months,—the leafy month of June,—breathing the sweet perfume of hawthorne, honeysuckle and wild rose, I listened to words sweeter to me than all their sweets combined,—to the words in which he told his love. This was the first day of June, 1850. Next day he returned to London to continue his interrupted studies.

If I had expected this consummation to my long cherished hopes would bring entire happiness, I was doomed to disappointment. Mr. Cornaby was not a believer, although he attended meeting punctually, and led a strictly moral life. I had refused other suitors on this very ground, and I keenly felt the inconsistency into which love was now leading me; especially as it was pointed out by friends, including my minister and adviser, who, in kindly earnestness, told me, that "loving him would take me to hell." In an instant, the words seemed put into my mouth, "If loving him will take me to hell, I shall go." Mr. F——, finding my decision was taken, said no more; but my conscience troubling me much, I at length took the whole burden of my sorrow to my Father in Heaven, until the guidance I had never sought in vain, came in the words, "This is the way, walk ye in it." I was satisfied, and regardless of consequences, walked the path, in which, without any choice of my own, I was being led. Shortly afterwards, Mr. Cornaby took a relapse; and London life, with its ambitious hopes of a profession, were alike abandoned. This was a great trial to him at the time; but He, who controls the destinies of the inhabitants of earth, was overruling all for his good.

Leasing a place in Great Yarmouth, Norfolk County, Mr. Cornaby opened a book store and, besides, gave lessons in phonography; thus finding occupation which, although not altogether to his taste, promised a livelihood; and on January 30th, 1851, we were married in St. George's Church, a venerable structure, celebrated for its antiquity and architectural beauty.

CHAPTER III.

The Light of the Gospel.

AMONG the current literature of the day that, in the way of business, passed through our hands, was a series of tracts published by Chambers, one of which, entitled, "Religious Impostors," attracted our attention. After giving an account of various religious impostors, it concluded by giving a brief history of Joseph Smith; and a foot note on the last page stated that the editors had heard, since the pamphlet had gone to press, that Joseph Smith had been killed by a mob. They regretted to hear this, for the reason that his fanatical followers would regard him as a martyr, and the delusion would spread.

This was our first introduction to Mormonism. Soon after this, another book came in our way, entitled, "The Mormons, Illustrated," published by the Illustrated London News Company. It contained copious extracts from Col. Kane's Lectures before the Historical Society of Pennsylvania; also from Joseph Smith's teachings. Although the book was written to show the fallacy of "Mormonism," it made a deep impression on my mind. My husband and I read it together carefully and thoughtfully, and we arose from its perusal satisfied of the divine mission of Joseph Smith.

For some time previous to this, the foundation of my religious faith had been shaken. Accustomed as I was to read my bible, it was impossible not to see many discrepancies between the teachings of the religious sects and those of the Saviour; most of all, the lack of promised signs which were to follow believers.

Our minds were not at ease; we were removed from former associations, untrammeled by any religious obligation, and were determined to seek for truth wherever it could be found. With the bible as our standard, we concluded to take its precepts as our guide.

We often took long walks by the sea side, unseen, save by that eye that is ever over the righteous, and prayed and talked upon the subject that occupied so much of our thoughts. This struggle went on for months.

I remember, once, as we were walking beside the river Yare, I wished I was sleeping beneath the deep quiet waters, I was so weary of this struggle. A gloom, for the first time in my life, had over-shadowed me. I thought my Father in Heaven had forsaken me; but at length, out of the darkness came the assurance, " Fear not, for I am with thee ;" but as yet, I knew not that this, the darkest hour of my life, would usher in the glad beams of the " Sun of Righteousness" whose brightness would increase until the perfect day.

It was the beginning of February '52, on a cold stormy evening, that, looking out at the door to watch the progress of the storm, I saw a man sheltering under the awning in front of our store. I invited him to come inside for better protection from the weather, which he did, expressing his thanks, but assuring me that if I knew who he was I probably would not welcome him under my roof. I was startled at this, but replied that I had only done what was my duty to any fellow-creature under the circumstances. He then introduced himself, as George Day, a Latter-day Saint Elder, who had been sent to preach the gospel in that town. I remarked, that I thought we had ministers enough already to preach the gospel; he replied, none of them had authority to preach; but he had been sent with authority as the Saviour sent his disciples. I then hastened to call my husband, who received him courteously, and invited him to supper. After supper, he spent the evening with us, telling of the Latter-day work; we listened with great interest until bed-time. We procured lodging for him at a hotel near by, and he breakfasted with us next morning. Before he left, he made an appointment, at our request, to call again that evening and preach to us, we promising to call in our near neighbors to hear him.

All day emotions of hope and fear were battling in our bosoms. Could this wonderful news be true? Was God about to answer our prayers for guidance in this manner? Had we, by receiving this stranger, unexpectedly received the blessing of peace to our troubled spirits? We scarcely dared to hope, yet dared not to doubt. Evening came, and with it Elder Day and the friends we had invited. He preached and we believed, and thought it impossible for any one who heard it to do otherwise; but with our neighbors, it was different; they could scarcely refrain from abusing him and us, and called us fools for listening to such lies. We were astonished beyond measure at this, thinking they would be so glad; but we were too happy to be angry at such strange conduct. When Elder Day left, we gave him permission to make our house his home, when he had no other. This meeting caused a great hue and cry, and parsons and others coming to hear about this new religion, we could do little else than answer questions. It was such a sudden turn of affairs, we hardly knew what to do; our friends became enemies; we were persecuted and annoyed in many ways. Before this, we were respected and esteemed by many. Now, if we walked along the streets, we met no kindly greeting, but were pointed out as "Saints," and sometimes stoned. Others believed, and a few were baptized when Elder Claudius V. Spencer, then president of the Norwich Conference, came and organized a branch of the Church of Jesus Christ of Latter-day Saints, in the town of Great Yarmouth. Elder Spencer removed a few lingering doubts from my husband's mind, and he was baptized and confirmed. I, too, desired baptism, but the birth of our first child delayed it for a time. We placed the publications of the church in our store windows. These attracted considerable attention, and at the same time relieved us from answering so many questions. As soon as my health would admit, I renewed my request for baptism. A time was appointed to attend to this ordinance. I left my babe in the care of a nurse whom I could trust, and proceeded to a house near the sea-side, where we met to make preparations. We found the house surrounded by a mob, through which we with difficulty made our way, amid oaths and threats of what would be done if any attempt were made to go into the water. We waited until near midnight, hoping the crowd would disperse; but it had all this time been increasing, until it numbered many hundreds, and we feared violence, not only to ourselves, but to the family, under whose roof we were waiting.

Wearied of the delay, the master of the house thought of a ruse. He went to the door, and asked permission for his son to pass through the crowd to his boat, as he was a fisherman, and it was necessary that he should sail with the outgoing tide. My husband, previously dressed in the son's clothes, stepped out, and I followed in the darkness unnoticed. They soon discovered that their prey had escaped, and before we reached the water's edge, the whole horde was upon us; and my husband baptized me amid a shower of stones, and shouts of "duck him! duck him!" and such cries. Elder Day appealed for protection to the police, several of whom were present, but they said they could do nothing. We then made our way back, as best we could, followed by the mob; and, although the stones whizzed around us thick as hail, not one touched us, and we reached home in safety, thanking God for our miraculous deliverance; determined, more than ever, with the assistance of the holy spirit, to adhere—through evil, as well as good report—to the principles we had embraced. At the next meeting of the saints, I was confirmed, and knew for myself that the work was of God.

Although persecution continued, many attended our meetings, and a few were added to the church, until our branch numbered 27 members. A few weeks after our baptism, my husband, by the counsel of Prest. Spencer, closed his business in Yarmouth and removed to Norwich, to take charge of the book agency of the Conference; and to labor in other departments, for which his abilities qualified him.

We rented a house in Botolph Street; and selling off, at a great sacrifice, our stock of books and other things we should not need, sent our household effects by steamer while we journeyed by rail.

This was the beginning of June, two years from the June before mentioned; then, we had not even heard of this Latter-day work, now, we were identified with it, and our names cast out as evil for its sake; but, oh! how happy we felt, as we journeyed on; how unspeakably dear we were to each other! The trials through which we had already passed, purified our faith and increased our love.

Before adopting our new faith, we weighed the matter well, and counted the cost. We were not coaxed nor coerced, but did it prayerfully, thoughtfully and intelligently; and could say in the words of the Apostle Paul, "Neither count I my life dear unto myself, so that I might finish my course with joy."

On arriving at Norwich, we were warmly received and entertained by Brother John Spriggs and his kind hearted wife; also Sister Francis P. Teasdel and her son; and many other saints—too numerous to mention,—but whose names have been fondly cherished through a lapse of twenty-eight years.

In our new home, we enjoyed without persecution the fellowship and communion of the saints, together with the gifts and blessings of the Gospel, promised by the Saviour. Only for a few weeks, however, were we permitted to enjoy these delightful privileges; my husband's health failed, and, as travel had hitherto proved beneficial to him, he decided to take a business trip through the midland counties to recruit; while I, for the first time since our marriage, was left alone saving the presence of our darling little daughter, now five months old. I corresponded regularly with my parents and sisters, and invited them to visit me in my new home ; but they excused themselves, and I, knowing their prejudice to my new religion, understood the cause.

Almost daily, my husband wrote very cheery letters telling of his improved health. After he had been absent about a month, I was attacked with a violent fever ; and although the more distressing symptoms abated, through the laying on of hands by the elders, I continued very week and low.

In this feeble state, I longed for the society of my beloved parents; but as there was no direct conveyance to Beccles, I resolved to go by train to Lowestoft, to my husband's parents, and was accompanied by Mrs. Neslen. This journey, although carefully taken, brought on a relapse. My friends thought the doctor should be called in, but I objected, imploring them to call in the elders. To this, however, they were opposed, and, not presuming to insist, I made my way in the evening, to the house of father Samuel Neslen, only to find that he and brother John Coggle had gone some miles out of town to administer to a sick person. Greatly disappointed, I crawled back as best I could, supporting myself by the buildings and fences as I passed along. I reached my room, the fever raging, with just enough conciousness to wonder if I should die, yet desiring life. I knelt by my bedside, repeating the words; "O, Lord, help me," until a voice said, "From this time will I bless thee." These words were repeated three times. More thankful than I can express, I arose from my knees, retired to bed, and was soon in a peaceful slumber from which I did not awake until the sun was high in the heavens. I then found that the fever had entirely left me, the consequent weakness only remaining, and which a few days of sea-side life removed so that I was able to bear the journey home. Next day my husband returned, after an absence of nine weeks, well and happy. Shortly afterwards, I visited my parents, who received me tenderly; and showed such affection for our babe—their first grandchild—that my heart smote me for the sorrow I had caused those loving hearts. Our parting was a sorrowful one, although I did not then know that I should never see them again on this earth.

CHAPTER IV.
My Native Land, Farewell!

MANY of the saints in the Norwich Conference were expecting to go to the "Valleys" the approaching season. We also caught the spirit of gathering and felt that England was no longer our home; but this thought brought with it a severe pang; we tried although vainly to dismiss it, and when Prest. Spencer told us of his release from his mission to return to Utah, adding that he did not wish to leave us behind, we determined by the help of the Lord to follow his counsel. My husband went and advised our parents of the intended departure; and they, although believing us deluded, yet gave us their blessing and their prayers, with many substantial proofs of their undying affection.

Our last Sabbath in England having arrived, Miss Martha Harris, a very dear sister, was spending the day with us. To divert our minds from the thoughts of a separation, my husband opened the parcel of *Millennial Stars* that had been received the previous day from Liverpool, and to our astonishment found the revelation on Celestial Marriage. We had a testimony that it was from God, and rejoiced that He had indeed restored the Gospel as in former dispensations. No principle or doctrine of our faith had been received by us with so much joy, as this heaven-born revelation. The testimony we had received of its divine origin, was a great blessing to us and others; for we had frequent opportunities, on board the vessel, of defending it to those who, not understanding it, were opposed.

The Norwich saints were notified to go in the first vessel which would sail that season; and as Prest. Spencer and some others could not be ready until the second vessel sailed, my husband was appointed to take charge of the first company until an organization was effected on board the vessel, when Elder Moses Clawson, assisted by Elders George Kendall and Thos. Pugh were appointed to preside. On the ninth day of January, 1853, we left Norwich, after a stay of only seven months, during which time we witnessed a great outpouring of the spirit of God on priesthood and members, young and old. We had seen a miraculous display of the signs following those who believed, had heard speaking in tongues, and the interpretation of the same; the sick were instantly healed, and evil spirits cast out. We heard the brethren and sisters testify to the truth of the Latter-day work; and took with us assurances of its truth which intervening years, under every vicissitude of life, has not effaced. The love of God shed on our hearts, had made them warm with love to all the saints. We mingled in their social gatherings, associated with them in their homes, and received them in return; and had ample opportunities of observing the elevating and refining influence of the Gospel of Christ, in the daily walk and conduct of those who had embraced it. Interwoven with all these, are sacredly cherished memories of our associations with Prest. C. V. Spencer and his gentle, lovely wife, Georgiana, who, alas! all too soon for those by whom she was so much beloved, was called to a better world.

Inseparably connected with this happy time, were the occasions when we were guests under the hospitable roof of Mother Teasdel and her son, brother Samuel P, listening while Sister Teasdel told, among other incidents connected with the commencement of the Latter-day work in Norwich, of a dream in which she saw the man who would first bring the Gospel to Norwich; and how, long afterwards, she saw and recognized the same man on the street, in the person of Elder Thomas Smith; and, as directed by the spirit, accosted the stranger, telling him of her dream, and inviting him to her house; thus being the first to open her house to a Latter-day Saint Elder in the Norwich Conference. This may seem like digression, but I could not leave the subject without perpetuating these pleasing memories.

Our journey to Liverpool, and the incidents of the sea voyage are described in the poem, entitled "Crossing the Atlantic Ocean." After our arrival at New Orleans, we took passage on board the steamer, *Rob Roy*. Our voyage to St. Louis was unmarked by anything worthy of note. The season being too early for us to proceed up the river, we were compelled to remain in St. Louis several weeks. Our stay here was rendered quite pleasant by the kindness of brother Amos Fielding and family.

Many of the brethren procured work at the different employments suited to their varied abilities. My husband obtained work in the book-bindery connected with the *Missouri Republican* office, the money he thus earned enabling us to procure many little extras, in addition to the company allowance. We were traveling in what was called the ten pound company. When about to leave, the proprietors offered Mr. Cornaby great inducements to stay; but all they possessed would not have weighed a feather in the balance; Utah was our goal, and "On, right on!" our motto, and onward we went; although repeated delays, and travel by ox teams, did not afford a very rapid means of transit. While here, the second company of Saints arrived from England; and we learned with sincere regret that sister Spriggs had died at Liverpool on her way to Zion.

We proceeded from St. Louis to Keokuk, in the steamer *Kate Kearney*; arriving there late in the day, we were obliged to shelter for the night in a large warehouse on the levee, without any accommodation but that afforded by our luggage.

Next morning, we proceeded to our camp on the brow of a hill overlooking the Missouri River. Here we found our wagons and tents. We had just placed our baggage in the wagons; some were making awkward attempts at erecting tents while others were trying to place the covers on the wagons, some of which obstinately refused to reach over at both ends, when we were struck by a furious storm of wind and rain, accompanied by thunder and lightning such as we had never heard or seen before. The storm raged with such fury that we feared the wagons would be upset, and after the wind had subsided, the rain poured down incessantly three days and nights, our luggage and bedding becoming thoroughly soaked, and the camp ground ankle deep with mud. Under these circumstances, my second child was prematurely born. A serious illness followed, but through the mercy of God, and the tender care of my husband, I recovered. During our stay here of one month, awaiting the arrival of the oxen and cows for our journey, we became somewhat familiarized with camp life. Our introductory storm having ceased, and our clothes and bedding dried, we enjoyed the genial sunshine, and the beauties of nature. The surrounding country was delightful in the habiliments of spring. Wild flowers of great beauty and variety were profuse in the woods. Many of the brethren obtained employment. Our Scandinavian brethren, with characteristic industry and forethought, purchased trees from the owners of the neighboring forests, from which they manufactured a variety of useful articles. Time passed swiftly. All were busy preparing for the journey.

It was three years, to a day, from that memorable first of June before mentioned, when our oxen having arrived, we left Keokuk. I wish I could afford a page to a description of our starting. The oxen were wild, and getting them yoked was the most laughable sight I had ever witnessed; everybody giving orders, and nobody knowing how to carry them out. If the men had not been saints, there would doubtless have been much profane language used; but the oxen, not understanding "English," did just as well without it. But it did seem so truly comical to witness the bewildered look of some innocent brother, who, after having labored an hour or more to get "Bright" secured to one end of the yoke, would hold the other end aloft, trying to persuade "Buck" to come under, only to see "Bright" careering across the country, the yoke lashing the air, and he not even giving a hint as to when he intended to stop.

Through the previous exertions and skill of our never-to-be-forgotten friend, William B. Woods, our team was made somewhat tractable; and was hitched up for the start with very little trouble. Imagine, if you can, the operation of starting over one hundred ox teams, chiefly by men who had never done anything of the kind before; but through the controlling power and ability of Captain Cyrus H. Wheelock, even this was accomplished; and we performed the journey of four hundred miles from Keokuk to Council Bluffs, in one month and two days, reaching there the third of July. Our road lay through a broken, sparsely settled country, much of the way through clearings in the woods, the stumps of the trees still standing, and sometimes through swamps and morasses; but by the blessing of God, we performed the journey with but trifling accidents. At Council Bluffs we stayed a few days to make final preparations for our long, long journey across the plains. There we made our first acquaintance with Indians, purchasing some moccasins of them, which we found much more comfortable than shoes in dry weather.

We were enabled, by selling some of our surplus clothing, to provide ourselves with many little comforts, and even what were then considered luxuries. Among other things, we purchased a good supply of groceries, an extra tent and some cooking utensils, also a lamp and oil, which we used to good advantage when the train halted a few days for repairs, &c. My husband also procured a good outfit of fishing tackle, and being an expert angler, supplied our "table" with wholesome fish. By a little forethought and management, the daily routine of camp life was by no means irksome. I often think that the weeks spent crossing the plains were as full of instruction and interest as any part of our lives. Admiring nature, we had abundant opportunities of beholding its varied beauties. Especially did we admire the flowers,—growing in some places in great profusion—handfuls of which daily adorned the wagon and delighted our child, which was in the care of a sister, who was too feeble to walk. The delicious wild fruits met with at different stages of the journey were much relished, and afforded a wholesome variety to our diet.

In consequence of the wagons being heavily loaded, all who were able, walked. It was a very interesting sight each morning to see our company break camp; the long train of wagons stretching itself out like a huge snake and winding its slow length along the boundless prairies. Those on foot starting ahead of the train, presented a motley appearance in their travel-worn dress, walking in groups, chatting, singing, laughing, talking principles and politics, or passing jokes as the case might be, all care being left behind. Some might be seen rambling on the prairies gathering flowers, others picking berries; sometimes an inviting stream would present itself, when fishing tackle would be in requisition. Those who were expert at hunting would go in quest of game, and would sometimes supply our camp with fresh meat.

At night, when we camped, the wagons were drawn up in a circle for protection, also forming a corral into which the oxen could be driven to be yoked. The teams, being unyoked, were driven to grass by the herdsmen, who guarded them through the night. Our camp presented a busy scene, some gathering fuel (which consisted mostly of either "buffalo chips," or sage brush,) some bringing water, others building fires and preparing supper, or baking bread for next day's journey. After supper, groups could be seen around the camp fires, singing the songs of Zion, talking of bygone days, or the hopes of the future, until the bugle call for prayers, when all except the guards (for we watched as well as prayed) retired to rest.

After proceeding some distance, and grass becoming scarce, it was deemed wisdom to divide our train, and it fell to our lot to travel the remainder of the way under the captaincy of Elder George Kendall, our associations with whom have always been remembered with pleasure.

While traveling along the Platte river, through

the Sioux Indian country, buffalo were abundant. We sometimes saw immense herds of them, a short distance from our line of travel. Here we often met with Sioux Indians, who were quite friendly, and on one occasion, we camped near one of their villages, where we held a big pow-wow, smoked the pipe of peace, and paid them a tribute of sugar and flour for the privilege of traveling through their domain. We also purchased from them buffalo robes and dried meat. Reaching Fort Laramie, we made a short halt when many Indians visited our camp; the squaws being particularly anxious to exchange their commodities for groceries, &c. I remember one squaw in particular, who took quite an interest in our dear little daughter; measured her foot, and next day returned with a very tastily embroidered pair of moccasins which she placed upon her feet, refusing to take anything in payment.

During our journey we passed and repassed other companies of saints traveling to the "valleys," and we had an opportunity of exchanging news. On one of these occasions, we heard with deep sorrow of the death of sister Martha Harris.

As we neared the Pacific Springs, the pleasurable part of our journey came to an end; provisions became scarce, the grass failed, and many of our oxen died; some wagons were abandoned, and the contents cached, or buried; we also encountered some heavy snow storms at the Springs, when our buffalo robes came in requisition.

When at length, from the top of the Little Mountain, we caught a first glimpse of the "Valley," our delight and gratitude found vent in tears of unfeigned joy, and when, on the morning of the 12th of October, 1853, we emerged from the mouth of Emigration Canyon and beheld the "City of the Saints," we felt more than repaid for the nine months of travel, and all the hardships we had endured. We seemed to inhale the restful spirit of the beautiful city, spread out in peaceful loveliness before us. The neat adobie houses with their trim gardens, the crystal streams coursing along the sidewalks, giving life to avenues of shade trees, all aglow with the lovely tints of autumn, presented a picture that is indelibly fixed upon our minds, and which the greater magnificence of the Salt Lake City of to-day has not the power to efface. Everything we saw so far surpassed our most sanguine expectations, that we could say, in the language of the Queen of Sheba, "The half was not told me."

With these feelings we entered Salt Lake City, and encamped on Union Square; thankful that our lives had been preserved, and that now we could rest after our long journey; for I had walked the entire distance from Council Bluffs—more than one thousand miles!

CHAPTER V.

Manna in the Wilderness.

AS our camp life was over, my husband went in search of a house, and rented one near where he had obtained employment, in the Eighth ward. Here we met with Bishop Everett and wife, very kind persons, who enquired into our circumstances, and offered any assistance we might require. Everybody seemed so kind that we thought of the promise of the Savior, "There is no man that hath left house, or brethren, or sisters, or father, or mother, or wife, or children, or lands, for my sake, and the gospel's, but he shall receive a hundred fold now in this time; houses, and brethren, and sisters, and mothers, and children, and lands, with persecutions; and in the world to come, eternal life."

We remained in this ward only three weeks, Mr. Cornaby having engaged to teach school in the Seventeenth ward. We rented a log cabin, opposite the schoolhouse, soon making the acquaintance of Bishop Joseph L. Heywood and his amiable family, with whom a friendship was begun which has never since been broken.

Another pleasant memory of this time was the kindness of Judge Elias Smith—one of the school trustees—cheering us occasionally with a friendly call, or inviting us to his house; sometimes paying the teacher with his own means, when other funds were not on hand.

In the spring of the year 1854, Bishop Heywood organized a Sunday School, and appointed my husband superintendent. We felt so much at home in this ward, that we decided to settle here, and bought for the purpose a building lot on Arsenal Hill, a beautiful site that overlooked the city and almost the entire valley.

Besides teaching school, my husband was secretary for the United States Marshal, which enabled us to live comfortably, and our home being near the Tabernacle, we enjoyed the privilege of attending meeting there.

On the 29th of August, 1854, our son, whom we named Samuel Last, was born in the little log cabin. My husband was still teaching school, and I can remember what numbers of the scholars came to see our new baby—some bringing presents for him. I hope some of them will read this, and learn how pleasant it is to me to think of them after a lapse of twenty-six years.

In the spring of 1855, we built a house, and in July moved into it. Those who have passed through a similar experience can imagine, better than I can describe, our feelings the first day we spent under our own roof.

The small harvest of this year, (caused by the ravages of grasshoppers,) brought to the people fears of famine, which in the fall began to be felt. We tried to prepare for the impending scarcity; but building our house prevented us doing so. This made us feel anxious, but we knew that the Lord had promised to provide; and casting our care upon Him, tried, (as we were not actually suffering,) not to look into the future.

In October, our children were taken very sick, and, not being acquainted with the diseases of this country, we did not know how to treat them, but here the experience and kindly aid of Sister S. M. Heywood were invaluable to us.

All this time the famine was creeping on, making itself felt. It was a gloomy time, even bread becoming scarce. Flour was ten dollars per hundred pounds, and difficult to obtain at that price.

My husband's school term being ended, he presented his bills, but could obtain very little flour. He took a bill of six dollars to Prest. Geo. A. Smith, two of whose children had attended school; but did so rather reluctantly, knowing his incessant public labors.

But with great gravity, Bro. Smith told him he had nothing to pay him in but *flour*, adding that he would be compelled to charge *six dollars* per hundred. Watching Mr. Cornaby's countenance, he seemed much amused at the look of surprise and wonder depicted there.

This unexpected and providential supply, used with economy, lasted us the greater part of the winter.

During this time of scarcity, our beloved president, Brigham Young, encouraged the saints to faithfulness and dependence on our Father in Heaven; promising them in the name of Israel's God, that none who would live their religion should die of starvation.

We believed this, and in the weeks following, found that our daily bread was given us; though sometimes in a manner as miraculous as the feeding of Elijah by the ravens.

In March 1856, we commenced digging roots on the bottom lands of the Fourth and Fifth Wards.

These roots were a species of wild artichoke, and about the size and shape of a person's finger. Their whereabouts was indicated by a small withered spray, resembling dried mint. They tasted much like the cultivated artichoke, and were very wholesome. When boiled, and served with thickened milk or gravy, they were quite palatable, and we often made a meal of them, (without the accompaniments of meat or bread,) with thankful hearts. Sometimes visiting and receiving company on this fare, we enjoyed each other's society, and "talked of the good time coming."

On the twenty-first of March, we passed through the Endowment House. Those who have enjoyed the privilege, can appreciate the blessing it was to us at this time. Having left all for the gospel's sake, we were repaid a hundred fold. I recollect how happy we felt next morning, as we joined a company going to dig roots. The warm rays of the spring sun seemed to diffuse gladness all around; everybody seemed cheerful; I was as free from care as the birds; and like them, wanted to praise the Creator for all His goodness.

In April, Thomas Callister, (by this time Bishop of the Seventeenth Ward) organized a company to go to Provo, to catch fish for the ward. My husband was among the men chosen for this expedition. It proved a success, and was a great help to me as well as to the people generally. Measures were also adopted by all the Bishops to ascertain who had more than sufficient breadstuff to last until harvest; many families who had a surplus, observed the most rigid economy, placing themselves on half rations, and some, even on quarter rations, to help out those who had none. The surplus was disbursed by the Bishops to those in the greatest need, the owners being amply remunerated. Although many were reduced to great extremities, no one died of starvation. Before leaving, he planted a few early garden seeds; others did the same, and it seemed as if the Lord blessed the people in this respect. Even the early salads gave hope, until more substantial vegetables would be ready. I remember how contented I felt, from day to day, if only my children had enough to satisfy their need; but it sometimes happened that the last morsel was eaten, with no prospect of another meal before us. The children, sometimes hungry, and beginning to understand the value of prayer, would coax me to pray to our Father in Heaven to send us bread; and I, feeling most anxious that my darlings should not lose confidence in prayer, would plead with great earnestness, they lisping the words after me. Many times the prayer was answered almost immediately, as the following instances will show.

It was evening, I was just preparing the little ones for bed, when my daughter, Edith, asked what we should do for breakfast. I told her not to think about breakfast, as she had had supper, and was not hungry then; but *she* reasoned that we had better tell the Lord that we had nothing for breakfast. So kneeling down with them, one on either side of me, I told our Father what we needed, and was just putting them to bed when a knock summoned me to the door. A neighbor came in with a large parcel in her arms and said that she wanted to write a letter to her husband, then on a mission to the Sandwich Islands; not having writing materials, she had come to see if I could supply her with some and offered, with apologies, a loaf of bread in payment. I supplied sister P—— with what she wanted, and she departed, satisfied and pleased, leaving me more thankful than words can describe.

Oh, what a loaf of bread that was, so large and light! The joy of the dear children knew no bounds. We thanked God, knowing that for many days we should not be hungry.

I trust to be forgiven for adding another circumstance to that just related. One morning having, as usual, attended to family prayer, in which, with greater significance than is often used, we asked, "give us this day our daily bread;" and having eaten a rather scanty breakfast—every morsel we had in the house—Edith was wondering what we should have for dinner, and why 'Pa did not send us some fish. I, too, was anxious, not having heard from Provo for some days; so telling my darlings I would go and see if sister Ellen Jackson, (whose husband was also one of the fishing party,) had heard any news, I started off. Sister Jackson had not heard from the fishery; but was quite cheerful, and telling me how well her garden was growing, added that the radishes were fit for use, and insisted that I must have some. It was good to see something to eat; and, quite pleased, I bade her good morning. Passing, on my way, the house of brother Charles Gray, sister Gray asked me where I had got such fine radishes. I told her, and offered to divide with her, to which she agreed, providing I would take in exchange some lettuce and cress, of which she had plenty. She filled a pan with these; and I hurried away thinking how pleased my children would be, if only we had bread to eat with them. As I was passing brother Simon Baker's house, sister Baker saw me, and invited me in. I told her I had left my children, and could not stop. She then asked me where I had got such nice green stuff, and when I told her, and offered her some, she replied, "if I would exchange some for butter, she would be glad." She then gave me a piece of nice fresh butter, which had just come from their dairy on the Jordan; and also a large slice of cheese. If I only had bread, I thought, how good these would be! Just then my eyes rested upon a large vessel full of broken bread. Sister Baker, seeing I had noticed it, told me its history. It had been sent the day before, in a sack, to the canyon, where her husband had a number of men working. On the way it had fallen from the wagon, and been crushed under the wheel. She did not know what to do with it, remarking that she would offer me some of it but feared I would feel insulted, although assuring me it was perfectly clean. I accepted her offer, when, filling a large pan, she sent her daughter home with me to carry it.

The children were watching for my return; and when they saw the bread, they clapped their hands with delight. Bread, butter, cheese, radishes, lettuce and cress! What a dinner we had that day! Elijah never enjoyed the dinner the ravens brought him, more than I did that meal; nor more fully understood that a kind Providence had furnished it. I could relate many other circumstances of a like nature, and even more remarkable—how wheat had been increased in the bin, and flour in the sack—but these instances will suffice to illustrate the providences of those times.

In June, the early vegetables helped our scanty supply of bread; and in July my husband returned, well and hearty, after nearly three month's absence. He had much to tell of his experience during those three months; having lived almost entirely on fish; the standing dish for the camp being fish soup (mostly suckers) made in a large iron pot, to which a little bran, or sometimes shorts, was added, the latter quite sparingly, as it could only be obtained as a favor at ten cents per pound. As this compound settled to the bottom, each one would take a dipper and give it a vigorous stir, to enable him to obtain his share of the floating particles. To this would sometimes be added a mess of boiled greens, gathered from the banks of the river. Very rarely, however, a few pounds of flour or corn meal were obtained and added to the repast.

The crops this season were early and plentiful; and on the twenty-fourth of July, my husband purchased a bushel of new wheat, and had it made into Graham flour. From this I made the first loaf of bread since the early part of February; and we had the assurance that the famine was over.

CHAPTER VI.

Pioneer Difficulties.

ON the 27th of July, while rejoicing in the prospect of coming plenty, we received an increase to our family, in the form of a lovely infant boy whom we named Henry.

During my husband's stay in the country, he had seen the advantages of owning land and raising grain for ourselves, without having, as in the City, to depend upon others. In a few weeks, he started for Spanish Fork to seek a new home; having heard while in Provo, of the advantages it offered to new settlers; namely, plenty of land, with a good supply of water. This was in August, 1856.

He attended meeting there on Sunday in a bowery (the only place of worship) erected on the public square. To his surprise, he here met with an old friend, with whom he had been associated in the 21st Quorum of Seventies, in Salt Lake City—William R.

Jones, who was leading the choir. Service over, brother Jones introduced him to the members of the choir. Shortly after he became a member of that choir, with which he is still identified, and brother Jones is still the leader.

During a period of twenty-four years, the Spanish Fork choir has been faithful in singing praises to God in the house of worship, also in times of mourning; and in the social gatherings of the people. Our departed president, Brigham Young, and also members of the quorum of the Twelve Apostles, have, at various times, eulogized and blessed this choir. I pray that that blessing may still attend it in the future and that members and leader may continue united and faithful to the end, and join in singing the songs which none but the redeemed can sing.

Bishop John L. Butler, who was presiding in Spanish Fork, seemed quite anxious that my husband should locate there; offering inducements, and helping him to select a building lot. The Bishop's fatherly manner, and the meeting with friends and kindred spirits, turned the balance in favor of Spanish Fork as our future home.

On the 26th of October, 1856, we left Salt Lake City, with all its advantages, to "rough it" in the country. For a time we felt the change very much; and especially did our children, who would cry to be taken home. Spanish Fork was a new settlement, having been but recently surveyed for a town site, and at this time, consisted principally of large wheat stacks, temporary dwellings, and houses in course of erection. The huge wheat stacks had a great attraction for us, who had so recently passed through a famine.

We rented a house, purchased a good building site, and built a small room in which to winter. This had just been accomplished, when my husband was taken very sick; but recovered in a month sufficiently to take a journey to Salt Lake City on business. He had but just reached his destination, when unfortunately he took a heavy chill and became entirely prostrated by rheumatic and lung fever. He was staying in the First Ward with friends, however, who kindly cared for him for many weeks, by which act they bound our hearts to them in gratitude. Meanwhile, I had remained in ignorance of his sickness, daily expecting him home,—the letters sent to inform me of his condition, not reaching their destination. My situation all this time was by no means enviable. The weather was very cold, and our temporary house afforded but poor protection from its severity. Mr. Cornaby, expecting to return in a few days, had left but little in store, and it was soon exhausted. With three helpless children, I had much need of fortitude, but was never left without a resource—my trust being in Israel's God, who has never failed me.

The recent famine experience had taught me economy, and the little I could procure from the sale of some clothing, enabled us to live. I could have made our condition known, and have received help, but delicacy forbade; so I made the best of the situation, exerting myself unceasingly for the helpless little ones.

Christmas Eve came, and my darlings, with childish faith, hung up their stockings, wondering if Santa Claus would fill them. With aching heart, which I concealed from them, I assured them they would not be forgotten; and they fell asleep with joyful anticipations for the morrow.

Not having a particle of sweetening, I knew not what to do. They must not, however, be disappointed. I then thought of some squashes in the house, which I boiled, then strained off the liquid.

that, when simmered a few hours, made a sweet syrup. With this, and a little spice, I made gingerbread dough which, when cut into every conceivable variety of design, and baked in a skillet, (I had no stove,) filled their stockings and pleased them as much as would the most fancy confectionaries.

I sometimes wonder if the children of to-day enjoy the costly Christmas presents of toys and rich candies with which they are surfeited, more than my little ones did their gingerbread toys, twenty-four years ago.

At this time, I received a letter from a friend in Salt Lake City, informing me that if I wished to see my husband alive, I must go to him at once; but the difficulties in the way seemed almost insurmountable. The roads were nearly impassable for snow. I was sixty miles from Salt Lake City. The only regular conveyance was by mail wagon, once a week. On applying to the mail carrier, he refused to take me; giving as a reason, the impossibility of a babe enduring the cold and necessary exposure of such a journey.

I sought the aid of Bishop Butler, who tried to dissuade me from taking the journey; but finding that I was determined, if possible to go, told me that in a few days some ox teams would go to Salt Lake City with tithing grain; but added that the journey would be attended with much exposure and danger. This delay was terribly trying; but I was compelled to curb my impatience as best I could. This was the time known as the Reformation Winter. Meetings were frequently held in private houses, and were termed Block Meetings, at which the gifts of the gospel were much enjoyed such as speaking in tongues, interpretation, and prophesying. These meetings were a great solace to me.

New Year's morning dawned, with the snow so

PIONEER DIFFICULTIES.   47

deep around our dwelling that I could scarcely make my way outside. A meeting would be held that day at the next house, on the same block, to which I wished to go; but found it would be impossible to get even this short distance.

While pondering over this difficulty, brother John P. Chidester called to tell me of the meeting, offering to carry the children if I wished to go, adding that his wife, Susan, expected us to dinner after the service.

Of course I went to the meeting, which was no sooner opened, than the presiding elder, Father John M. Chidester, directed his words to myself; and by the spirit of God, uttered a prophecy in which he told me that my husband was alive, and that the crisis of his sickness was past; that he would live to return home; and that for many years we should enjoy each other's society. I knew by the same spirit, that what he said was true, and my mind became easier.

On the third day of January, 1857, the teams started for Salt Lake City, and I with them; having arranged to leave my two eldest children in the care of sister Isabella Rockhill. The first day we traveled twelve miles, reaching Provo at dark. Greatly to my surprise, I met brother John B. Milner, with whom we became acquainted in crossing the ocean on board the "Ellen Maria." He, with his wife, made me welcome for the night, offering the best accommodation their house afforded. The following night I spent at Lehi, at the house of Elder Robert Winter, my husband's brother-in-law, who accompanied me next day on the journey.

I must mention a very providential deliverance I had that day. We had to pass what is known as the "Point of the Mountain"—the divide separating Utah and Salt Lake Valleys. The ascending grade made it impossible for the teams, six in number, to travel without doubling. This slow operation rendered it very tedious sitting so long in the wagon; and I became so benumbed, that, following the advice of the teamster, I dismounted and walked on, with my babe well wrapt; but the piercing wind and blinding snow made it hard work; yet necessity compelled me to walk fast to keep from freezing. This took me so far ahead of the teams that I did not know what to do. I attempted to retrace my steps, but was met by the wind and drifting snow, which I could not face; so continued on. At length I became so exhausted, I thought I must sit down; but knowing this would be death, I prayed to God for help and waded through snow, drifted so deep in some places that it was impossible to trace the road. Stupified and benumbed as I was, I wandered into a ravine, sinking down into a deep snow-drift, which nearly covered me.

I had just enough conciousness to wonder whether my babe was alive, and how long it would be until the teams would find me, when a stupor came over me, from which I was aroused by a kindly voice, and saw a horse's head quite close. A man passing with a sleigh, had seen me, and was trying to lift me out; yet fearing his assistance had come too late. He helped me into the sleigh, and drove to a house about two miles distant. By the time the teams came up, I had quite recovered. My babe was in deep sleep, and had not suffered.

We stayed at Draperville that night. Next day, Mr. Winter went ahead of the teams, to inform my husband of my coming, and sent a sleigh to meet me.

I found him very sick, but the worst was over; and in six weeks from that time he was sufficiently convalescent to return. On reaching home, we found the children all right. They had been well cared for in our absence.

Spring had set in; my husband, as soon as able, taught the Ward school; we spent the summer very comfortably, and began to enjoy country life.

In November of this year, our beloved Henry was taken away from us by death. This was a great shock, but we were taught submission to the will of Him who had given, and had the right to take away.

As the winter approached, considerable suffering for want of clothing was felt among the people, as there were no stores, and Johnston's Army, now on our borders, cut off all chances of supplies from the East. Many of the brethren having to endure the severity of the winter in the mountains, scantily clad, guarding their homes and families from an invading army, the sisters with true devotion supplied their wants from their own scanty wardrobes, in many instances converting their shawls into overshirts, and carpets into pantaloons! In those days a buckskin suit was something to be proud of.

In the spring of 1858, the "Move" commenced; when all the people living north of Utah County, removed south. This made our little town quite lively. Several families encamped upon our lot, constructing temporary shelter for themselves. The government, having been misled by mischief-makers, thought it had made a mistake; so sent commissioners to Utah to find out what was the matter with the Mormons. On inquiry, it was found they were "right side up," so they proposed to forgive us if we asked their pardon for keeping them out in the cold all winter, which we did with a very good grace, they promising to be quite peaceable if we would let them come in. The army entered our peaceful valleys and encamped at Fairfield, not as an invading force, but restricted and shorn of its power; bringing with it, money, clothing, provisions and supplies of almost every description, which were placed within easy access of the people. Thus the army which threatened destruction to us as a people, like so many of the efforts of our enemies to destroy us, only proved a blessing in disguise, and the wrath of man was made to praise the Lord. In July, the people returned to their homes in peace. We prospered temporally, and enjoyed the blessings of life as well as the consolations of our holy religion.

In January, 1859, our third son was born, whom we named Walter. This sweet babe only gladdened our home five months; then, after a few hours' sickness, the first his short life had known, passed away June 9th.

At the time of his death I was prostrated by rheumatic fever, and unable to wait upon him; but we had plenty of kind friends who were ready to help in this time of need. My lameness continuing, I followed the counsel of bishop Butler, was baptized for my health, and was soon entirely healed, giving glory to God for His mercy toward me.

For a time I was quite disconsolate over this second loss; and felt very anxious to know why my children had been taken from my keeping. I besought the Lord very earnestly in prayer; and one night, when, with strong cries and tears I had pleaded long, a promise came assuring me I should know why my children had been taken away.

The same night, the answer to my petition was given to sister Margaret, wife of brother Chas. W. Leah of this place. It satisfied me, and I have not shed a bitter tear on their account since. She arose from her bed, and wrote the words the spirit dictated; which are as follows:

> Peace to thy soul, my sister dear,
> The Spirit gently whispers now,

Come, wipe away the falling tear,
And chase the sorrow from thy brow.

I know the pangs that rend thy soul,
Thy tender offspring now are fled
To dwell around the Savior's throne;
Like stars they'll glitter on thy head.

The gentle buds bestowed on thee,
Have gone from this vain world of grief,
Their spirits could no longer stay,
But they have found a sweet relief.

With watchful care both day and night
A tender mother thou hast been,
Thou shalt be crowned in endless light
With all the graces of a queen.

May gentle peace her wings spread o'er
Thy dwelling from this very hour,
And give thee strength the race to run,.
Upheld by God's almighty power.

CHAPTER VII.

Miraculous Healing

ON the tenth day of April, 1860, our beloved bishop, John L. Butler, was taken away by death. He was succeeded by Albert K. Thurber, his first counsellor. Geo. W. Wilkins, his second counsellor, continued to act as counsellor of Bishop Thurber, and during the latter's absence on a mission to England, presided over the ward. He has been a near neighbor twenty-four years, and a true friend in our joys and sorrows.

The first of July of this year our hearts were cheered by another precious gift, our daughter Mary being born.

The following three years were noted only for the peace and happiness they brought us. The blessing of the Lord attended us and all we did, seemed to prosper. I have often thought that the storm tossed mariner could not enjoy a safe haven of rest, more than we did those years of calm and sunshine. During that time we had no sickness in our family, and the trials and sorrows of the past had been a great blessing to us in enabling us to appreciate the present. Our children were affectionate and obedient, our baby Mary was a real sunbeam, and our cup of happiness seemed full.

On the 4th of November, 1863, another daughter was born to us. She was a fine healthy babe, and no words could describe the joy of our household at this event.

At this time the war between the North and South was raging, and the papers were full of its horrors. My husband, knowing how apt I was to sympathize in such calamities, avoided any allusion to it; but one day a neighbor inadvertantly read to me an account of a terrible battle that had just taken place. It was more than I could bear in my then weak state and I took a chill, which was followed by fever, and for many weeks a struggle between life and death ensued; but when the bright spring time came, I was able to leave my sick room, and mingle once more with my family.

Not being able to attend fast meeting, Bishop Thurber and other elders came to my house, and we named our treasure Grace, Emily, Lydia. We called her Grace, no other name seemed so suited to our darling.

In September, when she was ten months old, she was suddenly taken very sick. We called in the elders, and administered mild herbs according to the word of wisdom, but all in vain. Our Grace faded away like a sweet autumn flower touched by the hand of death.

On the 27th of October, 1864, she was taken from us. Like David of old, while she was sick, we wept and fasted and prayed; but after she was gone, like him, we reasoned, we shall go to her, but she cannot return to us; and resolved not to displease our Father in Heaven by repining over this loss, we set to work to gather up the broken threads of life, and to provide for the comfort of the dear ones still left us.

A week after her death, and while diligently employed, I was suddenly prostrated by sickness, the like of which I had never known. At first we hoped it was only from the heavy strain my system had lately endured, and would soon pass off. We did all that wisdom dictated, and all that the love and affection of my family and friends could devise, yet with but short intervals, this debility and weakness lasted nearly six years. During all this time I was only able to attend public worship three times. This absence was a sorrow to me, as I feared to lose the spirit of God, but the assurance came, "My grace is sufficient for thee; for my strength is made perfect in weakness;" and like Paul I could say, "Most gladly, therefore, will I rather glory in my infirmities, that the power of Christ may rest upon me."

Soon after my sickness commenced, the gift to write in verse was bestowed upon me in a much greater measure than before, which was a great comfort, often making me forget my sickness and consequent weariness. In the beginning of the year 1870, in answer to prayer, the fainting spells that had been the most trying symptoms of my affliction were removed from me. I resumed my duties to some extent, and felt more hopeful than I had done for years past. The month of June having come, our garden was lovely with roses and pinks, and on the nineteenth day of this month, I remember how happy I was in the enjoyment of these beautiful gifts of nature. This day is more vividly impressed upon my mind from the fact that it was the last time for four years, that I had the privilege of walking in the garden.

In the afternoon of that day, Bishop Thurber, accompanied by some brethren, called to see the silkworms which we were raising from eggs he brought from England, when he returned from a mission to that country, and in the culture of which he took a great interest.

Shortly after their departure, feeling tired, I laid down to rest; but on trying to arise, was conscious of a pain in my head so violent that I could not lift it from the pillow. I also experienced a strange feeling at the heart, and could neither move myself, nor bear to be moved. My suffering was so great, that I could not sleep, but during the night I had a vision.

A heavenly personage stood by me and asked: "Are you willing to suffer for your own good, and for the glory of God?" I answered that I was. He then said: "Thou shalt come out of this sickness unscathed in body, sound in mind, and thy hair shall not be changed." Before leaving, this wonderful visitor told me his name, and also assured me that although the heavens and earth might pass away, his word should not pass away. I believed every word he had spoken, and during the years of sickness which followed, seldom lost hope of recovery, although, through the weakness of the body, sometimes feared I should not hold out, but do not wish to weary my readers with a recital of those trying years; for trying they were, both to myself and family, although they endured it without repining, and ministered unceasingly to my comfort. Our daughter

MIRACULOUS HEALING.

Edith was married and living at Salem, three miles distant, but was often with us, doing all that a faithful daughter could do. Our son was attending the Brigham Young Academy at Provo part of the time; so my Mary became my constant attendant, and with hired help we managed from day to day.

Many friends visited me during that time, some from distant places, and a remembrance of their kindness has made their names most dear. Foremost of these is brother Wm. W. Jackson of American Fork, with whom we have been on happy terms ever since the famine. Substantial and many were the proofs of his kindness, and that of his family.

The ability to write diverted me from my suffering, however, and enabled me to comfort the bereaved and distressed. I was often invited to compose for public meetings, and although confined to my bed, the sentiments I have penned have corresponded with the principles taught by the speakers on these occasions, which was a great satisfaction to me, and a testimony that I was taught by the same spirit.

For a long time, Elders Zebedee Coltrin, John A. Lewis, Philip Sykes and others, visited me almost daily, administering to me and blessing me, which was a great help in sustaining me through my sickness.

All the Elders had the same testimony, namely, that I should recover; but it was often a matter for wonder that I was not restored. We had to learn that the time for my healing had not yet come, and that we had to wait patiently the Lord's time.

Bishop Thurber, always kindly anxious for my recovery, sometimes brought visitors to see me; and on one occasion, to my great delight, he came accompanied by Apostle Orson Pratt. This visit was most opportune. My body was very much enfeebled by nearly three years of heavy trying sickness, and my spirit was languishing, for medical men had said my health might be improved, but I would never be able to walk again. Brother Pratt drew me into conversation, in which I told him the sorrows that were weighing down my spirit, and asked why I had not been healed. He answered my questions by referring me to many passages in the Old and New Testaments, Book of Mormon, and Doctrine and Covenants; conversing a long time as I had never heard any one else.

His words, though very gently spoken, came with such power that I knew they were the words of God to me; and have comforted me ever since. Before leaving, he asked if I wished him to administer to me, which, of course I was most anxious for. Bros. Pratt, Thurbur, and my husband laid their hands upon my head, when Bro. Pratt blessed me in the name of the Lord. I am sorry his words were not recorded, although I remember much of what he said.

He told me I should yet arise from my bed, and stand upon my feet; that I should walk into the different rooms of my house; that I should again walk in the garden and enjoy the beauties of nature; that I should visit my neighbors, and enjoy their society; that I should again walk to the house of the Lord, join in the singing, and speak of the goodness of God in the congregation of the saints. He also confirmed upon me the gift to write—with many other gifts and blessings.

He said he knew by the spirit that all he had promised would be fulfilled, but did not know when, as the spirit did not testify—the promised blessing might come soon, or I might have to wait—meanwhile he counselled us to continue to pray and to call upon the Elders as often as wisdom dictated. Brother Thurber remarked that it seemed worth being sick as long as I had been, to be the recipient of such blessings.

After Brother Pratt left, his wife, sister Marion R. accompanied by sister Thirza Thurber, came and spent a few hours with me, completing one of the most heavenly days of my life.

After this, though my health did not materially improve, my mind was calm and happy; and if at any time I felt like yielding to doubt, reminders would come of the promised blessing. Although it was fifteen months after this when the Lord in His mercy saw fit to restore me to health, the time of waiting passed hopefully, knowing as I did that the words of the servants of God would not fall to the ground.

The tedium of the following winter was relieved by frequent visits from Bro. James Wilkins and wife, old time friends from Pahreah, who were spending the winter in Spanish Fork. Bro. W. sometimes administered to me with much faith, and always testified that I should recover.

In the spring of 1874, President Brigham Young taught the principles of the United Order. The beauty and perfection of this heavenly order was shown to me with all the benefits it would confer upon those who lived in accordance with it.

In May, a company of young men was called to work at a saw mill, in the United Order. My son was among the chosen ones for this labor. I knew that if I desired it, he would be excused, but I was too glad to find him willing to obey the presiding priesthood, to raise any objection.

The first week of his absence, I missed him very much, but my husband, and faithful Mary, did all they could for my comfort.

Sunday came, I felt very feeble in body and depressed in mind, when brother William H. Darger, our block teacher, came to administer the sacrament to me. He noticed that I was not as well as usual, and asked if I wished to be administered to before he left. My husband anointed my head with consecrated oil, after which they placed their hands upon my head, and as nearly as I can remember, Bro. Darger uttered the following words. "Thus saith the Lord thy God, inasmuch as thou hast received the United Order, with all thine heart, and hast not withheld thy son, even thine only son, thy faith is tried, even as was Abraham's, thou shalt arise from thy bed, and shalt stand upon thy feet." In an instant I felt the healing power in every part of my body. Several persons were present at the time, who also testified to the power that attended the words.

When brother Darger was leaving, he said; "You will soon be well." I replied that I knew I should. Both my daughters told me they felt that the time for my recovery had come. As it was late in the evening I did not say much, I was so astonished at this wonderful event, that I seemed overpowered by the greatness of the blessing that had come upon me.

Next morning, when alone with my daughter Mary, I told her I was well, and requested her to bring my clothes that I might dress and arise from my bed. She wished me to wait until her father came in, but I wanted no one except her with me. I then got out of bed, and with one hand laid upon her shoulder, walked six times the length of the bed. My darling child was so overjoyed, that she exclaimed with uplifted hands, "Oh! mother, give the glory to God, give all the glory to Him, for it is all His work!" and she wept for joy. My husband coming in at the time, was astonished, and joined us in thanksgiving to God.

Thus, after being confined to my bed four years, I realized the promise made to me at the commencement of my sickness. I arose from my bed unscathed in body, sound in mind, and my hair was not changed. Although the sickness had left me, I was quite feeble, but strength returned gradually. At different stages of my sickness it had been deemed wisdom to call in medical aid, but for many months previous to this I had taken no medicine, being convinced that it did me no good. In less than a month from the time of my recovery, I walked to the house of God, and attended the fast meeting—thus verifying the words of Elder Orson Pratt. After the service was over, Bishop Geo. D. Snell called together some elders who, with him, laid their hands upon my head, and blessed me, giving glory to God for my recovery.

CHAPTER VIII.

Conclusion.

FOR a few weeks I did but little except enjoy my happiness, there was so much to admire. Everything seemed to have changed in the past four years. I did not know the town, so many improvements had been made. I was like a child in my joy; having been so long dead to the world and the conventionalities of society, it seemed like commencing life anew.

My dear Mary had so much to show and tell me, that we were all in all to each other, but this happiness was too great to continue; already the hand of the destroyer was laid on our beloved child, who again became sick of an epileptic malady from which she had suffered before my recovery.

The attacks were so frequent as to threaten her life; but after a long period of agonized suffering, she was restored to us, and in September, was baptized with her father and myself, for a renewal of our covenants.

In the seven months that followed, her health improved, and the anxiety we had felt for her vanished. She seemed happy and grateful, entered into every pursuit of life very heartily, and *lived*, in the true sense of the word. There was so much earnestness in all she said and did, that in looking back to that time I sometimes think she must have had a premonition that her stay here would be short, for she reminded us of one having a journey before him, for which he is anxious to prepare. She often conversed upon the principles and doctrines of our faith so intelligently that we were astonished at the wisdom she possessed; and although apparently in good health, often talked of death as if it had no terrors for her. She was eager to perform every duty, and faithfully attended Sabbath School; was a member of the Relief, and Young Ladies' Mutual Improvement Societies; and would on no account neglect prayer, either at family worship or in secret.

During her affliction, which continued (at intervals) for two and a half years, her father twice took her to Salt Lake City for advice and change. In April she was again attacked with the fits, which quite prostrated her; but she had suffered so much at different times and had survived, that we did not think of death as being near; but on the morning of the first of May, 1876, at the time she had gone forth many previous May mornings to gather flowers, her spirit took its flight to that land where the flowers never fade.

Bishop Snell, with Patriarch Zebedee Coltrin and others had their hands upon her head at the moment of her departure, and Brother Coltrin dedicated her to God to come forth in the morning of the first resurrection. She passed away with a smile on her countenance indicative of the joy she felt in the prospect of the life on which she was entering. Her brother and sister, ourselves, with several of her young friends were present, and seemed to catch the heavenly benediction of the departing spirit; but to dwell on this scene would be to open wounds partially healed. Her sojourn on this earth was only fifteen years and ten months.

Sister Mary Ferguson, president of the Relief Society, and many other friends whose names are tenderly cherished, were with us in this time of trial. We committed her remains to the grave, and the numbers who attended on that occasion showed how greatly she was beloved. We were supported through this great trial by knowing that for a little while only should we be separated, and that her spirit, unsullied by sin, had gone back to the Father, to mingle with those of the just made perfect.

After our return from the funeral, the spirit dictated the following verses to our son, the only ones he ever wrote:

Weep not, dearest Mother, so noble, good and true,
Your darling child has only gone to prepare a place
    for you;
Her angel form to God has fled, she could no longer
    stay,
Shed not those bitter tears, but bless the happy day.

Dear Father, I know 'tis hard to lose your darling
    now,
But she in Heaven is happy, with bright laurels on
    her brow.
Her earthly stay seemed very short, her life was just
    begun,
Let us all prepare to meet her, when our earthly labor's done.

In the fall of this year I went to Salt Lake City, not as in '57, when the journey occupied four days, but this time by train, in four hours. We had the privilege of entering the Endowment House to work for our dead, and I was baptized and sealed for many of them; which was one of the blessings promised me during my sickness.

On another occasion, (a very solemn one) I visited Salt Lake City, to attend the funeral of our beloved President Brigham Young. When I returned, at the request of the editor of the Young Ladies' Paper, I contributed some verses, expressing my thoughts on that event.

I have several times visited American Fork, where the affectionate welcome that has ever awaited me from Bishop L. E. Harrington and family, the Jacksons, and numerous other friends, have made that place and people dear to me.

It is more than six years since I was healed by the power of God; and if not robust, my health has been measurably good, enabling me to some extent to attend to my domestic duties, and in the summer time to enjoy myself in the cultivation of flowers, raising silk, and assisting in our apiary. Although not able to take an active part in public life, I have attended meetings occasionally, and have spoken "of the goodness of God in the congregation of the saints."

Much of my life has seemingly been wasted by sickness; still the years I had fondly hoped to have spent in active service in promoting the Latter-day work, have not, I trust, been altogether unfruitful, I having had opportunities at home to testify to those who have visited me, of the sustaining power of God. One thing I have learned, and prize it more than gold or silver; it is contentment with my lot. I have never known a time in my life when I could supinely sleep, or waste a moment in hopeless sorrow.

CONCLUSION.

I see now the meaning of the promise made to me in the days of my youth, "I will hedge up *thy way* with thorns." My way has indeed been hedged up, and I have been led in a way which I knew not, yet I am satisfied that it has been the right way.

It has been a hard struggle to give back to the Father of their spirits, the sweet children that for a time were so precious to me; but my greatest consolation is in knowing that my treasures are laid up in Heaven, safe from the contamination of sin; and I have the satisfaction of knowing that the coming of the Savior is near, when those who sleep in the dust of the earth will arise, and with the faithful on earth, enter into the joys prepared for them before the foundation of the world.

Meanwhile, although our home is childless, our grandchildren often fill the vacant places, and their tender love and childish prattle fill the void in our hearts, which for a time we thought nothing could supply.

The memory of the famine, and other privations through which I have passed, serve to enhance the happiness of the years of comfort and plenty I have since enjoyed, and which still crown my path; forcibly reminding me of the words of Moses to the children of Israel, in the 8th chap. Deut., 2nd and 3rd verses. "Thou shalt remember all the way which the Lord thy God led thee, these forty years in the wilderness, to humble thee, and to prove thee, to know what was in thine heart, whether thou wouldst keep His commandments or no. And He humbled thee, and suffered thee to hunger, and fed thee with manna, which thou knewest not, neither did thy fathers know, that he might make thee know that man doth not live by bread only, but by every word that proceedeth out of the mouth of the Lord doth man live."

In conclusion, I would say it is now twenty-nine years since in my native land, I heard and obeyed the Gospel as restored by an angel to Joseph Smith, the prophet of this dispensation, and gathered to this land that I might hear a living prophet make known the will of God to His people. And have I been disappointed? No, a thousand times, no. Though Joseph was slain, and Brigham Young, his successor, has gone behind the veil, a living prophet still leads and guides the Latter-day Saints.

This Gospel with all the keys, gifts, and blessings of former dispensations is worthy the acceptation of every creature under heaven. To establish this great truth, our Prophet, Patriarch and many others have sealed their testimony with their blood. Many of our Elders are traveling without purse or script, bearing their testimony and gathering the honest in heart to Zion; others are laboring at home in the interest of the Kingdom of God.

Women, whose names are widely known as champions for our faith, are earnestly working in the same cause, and many others equally zealous, whose names are comparatively unknown are working for the same end.

I desire to add my humble name to the great cloud of witnesses to the truth of this Latter-day Work.

HANNAH CORNABY.

Spanish Fork, Utah, January 17th, 1881.

POEMS

CROSSING THE ATLANTIC OCEAN.

A Reminiscence.

In January, Fifty-three, we left our English home,
Determined, for the Gospel's sake, to Zion's land to come.
Our family was very small, its members numbered three,
Yet strong in faith of Israel's God, and full of hope were we.
'Twas not to us an easy task to bid old friends adieu,
To take a long farewell of those who always had been true,
To leave for aye, the cozy home we made but just before,
And take a last fond look of things we should behold no more;
The wind blew keen, as out we went into the cold gray dawn,
But keener far the chill we felt within our hearts that morn.
The stars were shining over us, but brighter in our breast
Was the star of hope that 'lured us on to the distant West.

But if our hearts were sore and sad, as through those
 streets we went,
To leave the land that gave us birth, was still our
 firm intent;
For in the soul's deep recess, we heard the spirit call
"Come ye out of Babylon, lest share ye in her sure
 fall."
We reached the station, took the train, and (shall I
 own it) wept
As we left behind that city which still in darkness
 slept.
The good train bore us safely on, no accident befell,
That night we spent in Liverpool at a Temp'rance
 hotel;
Next morn we heard to our delight, that just the day
 before,
A company from Utah had landed on our shore,
And we hailed with joy not easy told, a missionary
 band
Of elders, who had come to preach the Gospel in that
 land.
We breakfasted together, tried each other's hearts to
 cheer,
Talked freely of the distant land, so distant, yet so
 dear ;
They blessed us with their cheering words, from them
 we comfort drew,
If they had braved the stormy sea, could we not brave
 it too?
If they had safely crossed the plains, the inference
 was clear
That we might also cross them, nor the cruel Indian
 fear.
We parted from the elders, they to their labors sent
And we to engage our places, within the vessel went.
Securely moor'd beside the wharf, our chartered vessel
 lay,

And soon our little earthly all was safely stowed
    away.
Ellen Maria, the vessel's name, she'd carried saints
    before,
And we were told the master there, was Captain
    George Whitmore.

It being yet a week or so before she put to sea,
To spend the time as best we could, at liberty we'd
    be;
The vessel thence would be our home, at night we
    slept on board,
By day we sought amusement which the city could
    afford.
Saints met us here, who, like ourselves, to Utah meant
    to go,
In whose society the hours flew fast and pleasant too,
And ere we thought the word was given, that all on
    board must be,
The ropes were loosed, the sails were spread, and we
    put out to sea.
E'en now, tho' twenty years have past, I live that
    time again,
But how describe the sounds that rose, of mingled
    joy and pain,
While we our voices joined to bid our native land
    farewell
Which told that we were going to another land to
    dwell?
And while we sang, a loud sad cry above the music
    went,
Followed by sobs and wailing moans of terrible lament;
For it was then we learned, what before we did not
    know,
That a few Irish emigrants were in the hold below.
Their country! oh, their dear loved isle! so touching
    was their grief

That many hearts 'till then quite brave, in tears now
    found relief.
Alas! the time was very short that we could spend in
    woe,
For as the vessel started, we had something else to do.
The sobs and cries, and outward signs of grief soon
    passed away,
And like a suffering, weary child, within our berths
    we lay.
Three hundred and sixty-three, I believe our numbers
    were,
And of that number, very few did not sea-sickness
    share.
The mem'ry of those dreadful days and what we
    suffered then,
Is fresh and vivid in my mind, but far beyond my
    pen.
Thanks to the Lord, my husband not a touch of
    sickness knew,
But with sufferers all around, found work enough to do.
Nine days and nights the wind blew strong, the sea
    was very rough,
The vessel rocked. loose boxes flew, and tins made
    noise enough;
We could not sleep through all that time, for clatter
    night and day,
Still in the Irish Channel, 'mid surging foam and
    spray.
At length we think of eating; our provision chest is
    stow'd
With goodly things of all kinds, for medicine and
    food.
We opened this, with anxious hope, but oh! alas!
    alas!
I never, never can describe the het'rogeneous mass.
Oranges, pickles, arrowroot, preserves, potatoes, jam,
Apples, brandy, mustard, rhubarb, and boiled ham,

Mashed and mixed together, as if the only object were
To find how much destruction, could be effected there.
This discov'ry is a trying and a sadd'ning one to us,
But outside, and around things are indescribably worse;
One of the men, the sailors say, from the topmost rigging falls,
We heard the crash, the awful thud, which every heart appalls.
Some of our brethren, tenderly, take up the mangled form,
And, with the captain's free consent, our sacred rites perform;
The healing power is manifest, the sailor's life is spared
And through his ling'ring sickness, for his wants our brethren cared.
In that dread time, a babe was born, yet scarcely drew its breath
Ere the mother with her darling, lay in the arms of death.
Death! ah, what a feeling with this word ne'er fails to come!
And if on land, 'mong loving friends, within the quiet home
'Tis an unwelcome visitor, how much more so at sea,
With lack of all that mitigates its sad austerity;
On land, our dead in holy consecrated ground are laid,
By loving tender hands and hearts, the last sad tribute's paid.
We touch the dead with tenderness, as tho' they could feel pain,
And venerate the senseless form, now all that does remain,
At sea this feeling is perhaps more deep and more intense;

For there the mode of burial is different, the sense,
The feelings, all are wrung. The forms before us now
Are dressed with all the gentleness, the billows will
  allow.
The infant laid, as if asleep, upon its mother's breast,—
But oh! my heart is sick and sad, how can I tell the
  rest?
Canvas close around was sewed, then weighted at the
  feet,
The bodies on a board are placed; preparations are
  complete;
And the forms we lov'd and valued, alas! they soon
  must be
Committed to the merciless, the deep and yawning
  sea.
They now are borne upon the deck, with due sol-
  emnity
We follow them with feelings sad, the burial to see.
The dedicat'ry rites and prayer are by the Priesthood
  said,
And we proceed, with sorrow now, to bury these,
  our dead.
Reluctantly the board is raised across the vessel's
  side,
And being gently tilted, down the bodies swiftly
  slide
Into the open water; and now the rippling wave,
Receives them with a plash, then closes o'er their
  grave.
But there's comfort in the thought that God, our
  God, has said,
That yet the sea at his mandate, again will yield its
  dead;
And knowing that the God we serve, is truth, as well
  as love,
We bow to Him, who ruleth here, as in the realms
  above.

Then in confidence to our Father, and to our God we prayed,
That our lives might still be spared, and the roaring winds be stayed.
Then He who holds the winds as in the hollow of His hand,
To stop their raging fury, now in mercy gave command.

"Be still!" is heard, the wind obeys, and heavy billows lower,
We see Omnipotence displayed and wonder at its power.
We view the broad Atlantic, smooth, placid, still and calm,
Its waves are sporting harmlessly and gentle as a lamb.
The respite is most welcome; those who can, now walk on deck,
And note with wondrous interest, each distant moving speck.
The sailors, busy round the ship, repairing break or rent,
Captain and mates their orders give, all seem on bus'ness bent.

We meet our fellow passengers, and for the first time speak
To some who on the deck appear, though looking low and weak.
New life and hope inspired our hearts, and drooping spirits buoy,
E'en the dumb fishes seemed to leap, and manifest their joy;
We see our Irish neighbors, who again have ventured out,
But seem to be regarding us with fear, distrust and doubt;

They'd heard, of course, what dreadful folks these
　　Mormon people are,
And so it would be just as well, of them to have a care.
Two girls among them differ, and soon grow free
　　and chatty,
And told us of their brother, who lived in Cincinnatti;
That he had sent some money, and that all his friends
　　had come,
And now were on their way to make America their
　　home.
We learned that they are very poor, allowances are
　　bare,
But thanks to those who manage things, we've plenty
　　and to spare.
We therefore help them what we can, and often are
　　made glad,
To see the light of grateful joy, in eyes before so sad.

Peace on our vessel now prevails, order again re-
　　stored,
The daily prayer and praise ascend, like incense to
　　the Lord.
The stormy past is over, and it seems almost forgot,
The present with its duties, engrossed our every
　　thought.
This life at sea; ah! who can tell its ever changing
　　face?
Who from the mind the beauty of those sunset views
　　can chase?
How describe the stars at night, reflected in the deep,
Or yet the holy wondrous spells that o'er the senses
　　creep?
As easy could we count the sands that hold the mighty
　　sea,
Or penetrate the mysteries of a vast eternity.
All things around us seemed to blend, on all is
　　stamped sublime;

CROSSING THE ATLANTIC OCEAN.

As, in our thoughts we lift the veil, that shrouds the things of time.

That vessel was our little world, its inmates were a book,
And from it hist'ries could be read in every word or look,
We saw, as in a day-dream, its ever open page,
In those few, eventful weeks, which really seemed an age.
On, on, we go, forever on, yet never seem to speed,
For surely, if we go at all, it must be slow indeed.
Yet the sailor at the helm, says "we're moving fast and true,
" Ten knots an hour the vessel speeds;" and he's the one to know.

A young couple of our voyage, about this time decide,
To sail, henceforth, together, a life voyage, side by side,
Sunday dawns and on the deck we witness the marriage rite,
As the Priesthood, in holy bonds, this couple now unite.
We soon are conscious that we breath a warmer atmosphere,
A soft and balmy feeling comes, and other signs appear.
The monster whale, now daily seen, sends forth a cloud of foam,
And dolphins in their rainbow hues, quite near the vessel come.
The flying fish amuse us, as in shoals they fly or leap,
And seem at home in air above, or in the wat'ry deep;
The nautilus spreads its little sail, and skims the briny wave,
In praise to the Creator, who their various instincts gave.

While watching these, we seemed to lose the weary
  lassitude,
Which through the tedium of those days, would often-
  times intrude.
Two infant strangers came on board, a baby girl and
  boy,
Whose advent to our little world, made quite a stir
  of joy;
In compliment to the captain, the parents named
  their son,—
That boy and mother are alive, the girl and mother
  gone,
These only lived a few short days, and when we
  reached the bar,
With many tears of real grief, we left our sister there.
We're drawing near the islands now, and stormy winds
  prevail,
While sometimes in the distance, we descry a vessel's
  sail.
One now comes near, the captains through their
  speaking trumpets greet,
We learn that all are hungry, having nothing left to eat;
Our company has plenty, and is willing to divide.
The boats in haste are lowered, and are quickly
  brought 'long side,
She was from Charleston, outward bound, by storms
  had been delay'd.
Provisions now were handed out; all hurry while she
  stayed;
The scene was novel, all on board felt truly thankful
  then,
That we could save from suffering, those needy fellow
  men.

Just after this, I think it was, the discov'ry was made
That our frail bark had sprung a leak, and quick the
  tidings spread.

Hours of intensely painful fear, and dread suspense
 ensue,
The men all labor at the pumps, the water to subdue.
Pale sad faces now are seen, e'en Charley, our merry
 cook,
Seems to have quite forgotten his accustomed laugh
 and joke.
The second mate looked in, with expression droll and
 sorry,
"Well never mind," said he, "we all are going to
 glory."
At length suspense is ended, we are told the danger's
 o'er,
While joy and gratitude prevail, where all was grief
 before.
Again come calm and quiet, a little breathing spell,
Ere of danger to our vessel, once more I have to tell;
I'm writing this from mem'ry, o'er a lapse of twenty
 years
Of life's e'er changing phases, its mingled joys and
 tears;
Yet on memory's tablet they have been so firmly
 placed,
That reason must resign its throne, ere they could be
 erased.

Our vessel steers its course, near the Bahama Islands
 now,
The voyage, almost o'er, we're near the Gulf of
 Mexico;
And congratulate ourselves, while with hope each
 heart beats high,
Nor mark the distant storm clouds now gathering in
 the sky,
But those who guide the vessel can her fearful peril
 see,
A gale is coming; and she drives with strange velocity,

Heedless of helm or sail, on towards a treacherous coast,
And, unless her course is changed, she will certainly be lost.
Oh, the fury of that storm ! our ship will surely wreck,
The women are all kept inside, the men ordered up on deck,
We cannot see what's going on, but hear the deaf-'ning din
Of fearful noises overhead, the screams and cries within.
Anchors overboard are cast, to stay her dangerous flight;
The peril is augmented by the darkness, for 'tis night;
The anchors' weight like feathers seems; still on the vessel goes,
For her keel's quite near the sand, as each anxious sounding shows;
We know that there is danger, yet there's potency in prayer,
And in this trying moment, ask our Heavenly Father's care;
Our spirits feel its soothing power, and patiently we wait,
The few brief moments, which we know must soon decide our fate.
The captain, for a moment, comes inside the cabin door,
And in his face we read a look we never saw before,
He gazes on the passengers, but utters not a word,
Yet plainly then we learn our fate, altho' no sound is heard :
My husband now comes in ; his face looks pale, but calm ;
He sits down close beside me, takes our babe upon his arm ;

Then seeks, with tender loving words to know if I'm aware,
Unless Jehovah's power prevents, death must be very near.
We tell each other of our hope, beyond the reach of death,
Which will not fail us, even though we should resign our breath,
And though, perhaps, all human power is impotent to save,
Our trust is stayed on Him who can control the wind and wave.

The wind is hushed, the danger past, oh, how the tidings come,
To all who now expect to meet a sudden watery tomb!
Life comes to us instead of death; joy takes the place of grief,
But how describe the feeling of the wonderful relief?
The vessel righted, now her course again can be controlled,
And with the morning light the distant coast we can behold,
While now we shudder, as we think, what would have been our fate,
But for the interposing power, displayed for us of late.
We pass the islands near enough to see the huts on shore,
And the cook, with much importance, now tells us something more,
Assures us he is willing, on his Irish oath to swear,
That he can see the natives frying breakfast pancakes there.
We are talking now of the wonderful escape we've had,

When the second mate, with his ever ready humor said,
" 'Tis a good thing for us, that we'd a lot of Saints aboard,
Or we'd all now be in glory, if you'll believe my word."
All is plain sailing, soon we pass the Reefs of Florida,
And reach without more accident the often talked of "bar."

Here we must wait the length of time that often intervenes,
Before a steam tug comes to tow ships up to New Orleans.
We feel impatient, but must brook the tedious delay,
'Tis now the third of March ; our child is one year old to-day.
Our life on sea is ended, but the danger is not o'er,
A mighty turbid river, with its perils, lies before.
As we cannot now move forward, we'll go back in thought, and view
The pleasing, painful incidents, we've recently passed through.
Six weeks since, we took leave of the English river Mersey,
We are now at the mouth of the famous Mississippi.

In the past six weeks we have crossed the waters which divide
Two mighty cont'nents, and, thank God, are on the western side,
And so much nearer the dear home on which our hearts are set,
For Utah is our guiding star, our land of promise yet.
We sang the songs of Zion, as we crossed the briny deep,
In perils, sought God's care, who o'er His people watch does keep.

Felt how very strong the bond that binds the saints together,
Our faith, our hope the same, each is a friend or brother.

But all who started on this voyage, are not with us here,
The briny deep now rolls its waves o'er some who still are dear.
A little orphan girl, a kindly passing tribute claims,
Although unknown to me her hist'ry or her parent's names.
She pass'd away so gently, those around her only knew
Death's presence, by his impress stamp'd upon her pallid brow;
We could not weep, because we knew her spirit then had gone,
To enjoy a home prepared for her where sorrow could not come.
The casket, left behind, now 'neath the restless ocean sleeps,
Her minist'ring spirit, over it, unceasing watch still keeps
Until the time predicted, when the resurrecting word,
In the depth of ocean's bed, by the sleeper will be heard.

But the present calls us back, and forbids to linger more,
It has a scene as sad as that which was described before;
A sister now is dead; a loving wife and mother gone,
Her sun of life, alas! went down, before it yet was noon.

The "tug" is here; farewell sea, we're starting up the river,
Good bye, old Neptune, we leave your realms, perhaps forever.

We are on the Mississippi, how wonderful it seems,
And views of terra-firma now, unlike the poet's dreams;
How good the change of scene, and how welcome the sight of land,
With signs of life displayed around us on every hand.
How dif'rent the vessel's motion! she seems but just to glide
On these wondrous waters, unheeding either wind or tide,
O! this majestic feeling is really grand to me.
Who only knew such rivers as the Yare and Waveney,
The last named river was the idyl of my youthful days,
On its smooth surface, I have watched its ever winding ways,
Followed its quiet wanderings through meadows sweet with flowers,
Along its banks have rambled in my childhood's happy hours;
My sisters, my companions then, enjoyed those scenes with me,
And oft we 'woke the echoes, in our merry childish glee;
And later, he, with whom I sail o'er time's uncertain stream,
While boating on this river, awoke life's happiest theme.
'Tis night! I'm dreaming of my home, and happy English scenes,
But 'wake to find I'm far away; we're now at New Orleans.

'Tis early morn, and from our berth can wharf and
    houses see,
And genuine the burst of joy, we've reached America.
We thank our God for all the past; my husband
    goes on shore,
With feelings strangely new and glad, our breakfast
    to procure.
Returning, he brings water, molasses, and light
    warm bread,
Not sumptuous fare, but tasted, then, the best we
    long had had.
With our spirits light and gladsome, these viands
    seem so good
To us who long have only had, bad water and ship
    food.
The air seems to exhilarate, we feel so rich and free,
I question, if just then on earth, were folks more
    glad than we.
The vessel quickly empties of passengers and crew,
Of course all had to go on shore, New Orleans to
    view.
We ramble through the streets, and wonder at the
    air,
Half French, half tropical, which meets us every-
    where;
The French market was a marvel, with its show of
    fruits and flowers,
But a description of it baffles my poetic powers.
The buildings were magnificent and imposingly
    grand,
But of a style I had not seen within my native land.
I did not like the feeling there, and only take away
Three pleasant recollections which are cherished to
    this day.
A negress kindly gave an orange to my little child;
A lady handed her a bunch of luscious grapes and
    smiled;

And of some early flowers we bought, just gathered from the sod,
So pure and sweet, they might have come, fresh from the hand of God.
Here, as at Liverpool, the vessel is our only home,
And back to its kindly shelter, at night, like bees we come.
The time is drawing very near, when we shall have to go ;
To-morrow, we must bid the *Ellen Maria* adieu.

It seems as if but yesterday, since first we came on board,
Yet if recorded, what a page its log-book would afford !
Those events are on my mem'ry, and come before me now,
As, for the last time, I stand awhile upon the vessel's prow.
We have suffered, but how willing has been the sacrifice,
Which, like accepted incense, has risen to the skies.
Gratefully, our thanks ascend, to our Father, God, in heaven,
That to us in these Latter-days, He has the Gospel given.
Then we'll welcome all before us ; let tribulations come,
We are only pilgrims passing through them to our home.
But there's no more time for reverie ; we've orders now to go,
And make our acquaintance with the *Rob Roy* and its crew.
My first impressions still remain, I've kept them ever since,
And never hear a steamboat named, without a shrug or wince.

We must leave our Irish neighbors, who only thus
    far come,
T'escape from poverty, and make in this free land a
    home.
Now very hearty, almost tender, is the last good-
    bye,
That in the bustle of the hour, we just have time to
    say.

Captain, mates, and all the ship's company, here we
    must part,
But pleasant mem'ries of you, will go with many a
    heart.
The poor sick sailor, (our brethren's care) now is
    going off,
We see him on his crutches, slowly moving 'long
    the wharf.
Ellen Maria, old friend, we take our final leave of
    you,
Tho' dangers oft have threatened, you've borne us
    safely through,
Many the saints that you have brought, and landed
    on this shore;
But now adieu, ill-fated ship, you'll carry saints no
    more.
On her next voyage, this vessel, a total wreck was
    found,
Her captain, and the sailors all were saved ; not one
    was drowned.
On the steamer now ! as she is moving off we are
    told,
There are slaves on board, going up the river to be
    sold;
Orleans is rich with such traffic ; believe me when I
    say,
I'd rather own the faith I hold, than all its wealth
    to-day.

A SIMILITUDE.

Cast thy bread upon the waters, for thou shalt find it after many days.
Eccl—11—1.

Cast thy bread upon the waters,
And doubt not in thy mind,
For after many, many days,
The harvest thou shalt find.

This lovely little metaphor,
Used many years ago
By Solomon, is surely meant,
A hidden truth to show.

In Egypt's land where drouth prevails,
And rains but seldom fall,
Where, it would seem, that food for man
Could not be raised at all,

At certain times, the river Nile
Its banks will overflow;
And over all the land around,
The rushing waters go.

The people then go forth in boats,
The "bread"—or rice—to sow,
Which cast upon the waters round,
Sinks to the soil below.

The waters soon again recede,
Again the land is dry,
And now a lovely crop is seen,
To cheer the passers by.

And is there not a moral hid?
A truth which e'er will last?
A sense, in which upon life's stream,
Our bread may oft be cast?

A thought, a word, a deed of ours,
If broadcast sown around,
May yield a crop more precious far,
Than Egypt's rice when found.

A kindly word may sink below
The surface, and be hid;
But oh! it never can be lost,
'Twill rise again unbid.

It germinates in heart's deep soil,
A harvest of the mind
Will bless, and pay the sower's care,
And his reward he'll find.

A general harvest time will come,
Then, all that we have sown,
The good and evil, will be seen
And their results be known.

CONTEMPLATIONS.

And they that be wise shall shine as the brightness of the firmament; and they that turn many to righteousness, as the stars for ever and ever.
Daniel—12—3.

The mind that takes a wide survey on Contemplation's
    wings,
And calmly views this world of ours, and present state
    of things,
If filled with true philanthrophy, will feel the bosom
    glow
With warm desire to alleviate, the evils seen to flow.
Our world is old, and every age has light of reason
    brought;
Great minds have been employed, yet the philosophy
    taught,

Has only given to the world, just light enough to show,
That still in reason's light alone, error and darkness grow,
Priestcraft and kingly tyranny have made the nations groan;
And for the evils they have caused, are powerless to atone.
The sword has slain its millions, and o'er the hideous tomb,
The baneful weeds have grown more rank, because not overcome.
Thus, superstition, ignorance, crime, bigotry and pride,
Now are sweeping like a torrent, fearfully deep and wide.
What power can stem this surging stream, or bid its mighty wave
Recede, ere it engulfs the world in one huge common grave?
This question might be asked in vain, but happily we know,
A safer light than reason gives, has dawned upon us now.
The Priesthood of the eternal God, to man is given,
With Revelation's light to guide us back to God and heaven;
Yet great as are the evils still resulting from the curse,
Wide spread as are the miseries that fill the universe,
So ample is the remedy the Gospel's light has shed,
Embracing all of Adam's race, the living and the dead.
And human agency must help to carry out the scheme,
The immenseness of which will be eternity's grand theme.

To those who know the Gospel, in its purity and truth,

Belongs the all important work to educate the youth.
And those whose pleasing task it is to teach the rising age,
Will find encouragement and aid, on wisdom's written page.
The Bible, sacred volume! teems with promises to cheer
All those who strive with honest hearts and purposes sincere.
And is it not a noble work, to mould the youthful mind!
To break the chain which sin and vice around their vot'ries bind?
To bend aright the pliant twig, to train the growing bough,
That they like "trees of righteousness," before the Lord may grow.
Perhaps the teacher's hardest work, the real toil, is found
In combatting the traditions, which in this age abound.
To counteract their influence, is sure no common task,
But who is equal to this work? all earnest teachers ask.
Yet is there not sufficient to sustain us in the thought
That we are laboring to bring God's purposes about?
Tis ours in faith, where'er we can, to sow the seed of truth,
To God belongs the blessing so essential to its growth;
For steadily truth's light must shine, until it clears away
The fog and mist of ages, and reveals the perfect day.
Both ignorance and sin will flee, and knowledge, like a flood
O'erspread the earth, for prophets tell that all will know their God.

SONG.

WHO IS ON THE LORD'S SIDE?

Tune—Life on the Ocean Wave.

Who's on the Lord's side? Who?
Now is the time to show;
We ask it fearlessly,
Who's on the Lord's side? Who?
We wage no common war,
Cope with no common foe;
The enemy's awake;
Who's on the Lord's side? Who?

Chorus.—Who's on the Lord's side? Who?
Now is the time to show,
We ask it fearlessly,
Who's on the Lord's side? Who?

We serve the living God,
And want his foes to know,
That if but few, we're great,
Who's on the Lord's side? Who?
We're going on to win,
Nor fear must blanch the brow,
The Lord of Hosts is ours,
Who's on the Lord's side? Who?

Chorus.—Who's on the Lord's side? Who? Etc.

The stone cut without hands,
To fill the earth must grow,
Who'll help to roll it on?
Who's on the Lord's side? Who?
Our ensign to the world,
Is floating proudly now,
No coward bears our flag,
Who's on the Lord's side? Who?

Chorus.—Who's on the Lord's side? Who? Etc.

The powers of earth and hell,
In rage direct the blow,
That's aimed to crush the work.
Who's on the Lord's side?   Who?
Truth, life, and liberty,
Freedom from death and woe,
Are stakes we're fighting for,
Who's on the Lord's side?   Who?

Chorus.—Who's on the Lord's side?   Who? Etc.

The Lord has armies great,
Which at his bidding go,
His chariots are strong.
Who's on the Lord's side?   Who?
When he makes bare His arm
To lay the wicked low,
Then is the time to ask,
Who's on the Lord's side?   Who?

Chorus.—Who's on the Lord's side.   Who? Etc.

Then rally to the flag,
Our God will help us through,
The victory is ours,
Who's on the Lord's side?   Who?
Stainless our flag must wave,
And to the nations show
The olive branch of peace,
Who's on the Lord's side?   Who?

Chorus.—Who's on the Lord's side?   Who? Etc.

CHRISTMAS IN MY CHILDHOOD'S HOME.

A Retrospect.

Christmas—whatsoever the cynic may say
To me, is a welcome and bright holiday,
Bringing back memories I ne'er would forget;
Thro' the mists of the past, that spot is green yet.

On Christmas at home, when mother's loved voice
Would tell us the reason why all should rejoice.
We listened with joy, though the tale was the same
How shepherds, to herald the glad tidings came.

That Jesus, our Saviour, in Bethl'em was born,
And the angels rejoiced on that auspicious morn,
That peace and good will towards man was the strain
And the heavenly host caught up the refrain.

With what rapture still, does memory go back,
Forty long years, over life's uneven track,
To childhood's bright days, and my dear happy home,
Where my sisters' loved forms like sweet pictures come.

Christmas eve! what a host of thoughts it can bring,
And fond recollections around it still cling,
When my father brought home the bright holly bough
With laurel and ivy, and famed miseltoe.

E'en now comes again the glad bustle and hum,
Over time's heavy mist, the sound seems to come,
'Twould be midnight e'er decorations were made,
And tired, happy children, our good-nights had said.

Next morning it seemed that we scarcely had slept,
Ere merry Christmas chimes o'er sleepy ears crept,
We dressed, ate our breakfast, then hastened away
To the church, where service was held on that day.

That church! I suppose it would not be amiss
To give just a word to that grand edifice;
The structure was old, by the Catholics reared,
'Twas plain that no labor or cost had been spared.

Its groin'd and arch'd windows were marvels of art,
The crucifixion of Christ on one formed part,
The colors, subject, and conception sublime,
Remaining unchanged by the touches of time.

Were my powers of description greater, I might
Describe things inside, which inspection invite,
The walls filled with tablets of marble that told
How hearts, once quite famous, have long since grown cold.

The ten commands graven on tables of stone
The "Lord's Prayer and Belief," I've read every one.
Have knelt on the grand marble steps, that then led
To the altar, where holy emblems were spread.

Then the grand organ, with its deep solemn sound
Awoke veneration, and worship profound.
The organist, too, seemed a part of the whole,
As did also the blower, poor, lame, old John Bull.

But why linger thus, for you wanted to hear
How Beccles church look'd in its holiday gear;
When various employees had all done their best
And in bright green and red the old church was dress'd.

Well then, 'tis with shame that I now have to own.
More respect to the church, than parson was shown.
We admired the bright green and the berries so red,
But scarce gave thought to what the minister said.

The old place looked grand, and we counted each spray
That on pulpit, desk, and on chandeliers lay;
And were anxious to see whatever came next,
But alas! not once thought of lesson or text.

No doubt this was wrong, and you'll not be surprised
To hear we looked foolish when next catechised,
But perhaps we all learned the lesson conveyed,
In the words of reproof the rector essayed.

But no thought of this passed through our heads that day,
And when service was o'er, we hurried away
To our home, where we found the table was spread,
Roast beef and plum pudding, in holly arrayed.

Dear mother helped quickly to take off our wraps;
Pellices and shawls, gloves, bonnets, hat and caps,
For the nonce, were all left heap'd up in a pile,
As the dinner was getting *cold* all the while.

We quickly were ready, the blessing was asked,
And all set to work on the Christmas repast.
I own on the whole, ample justice was done
To the viands 'mid plenty, talking and fun.

Then, after dinner, there were dried fruits in store,
Hid safely away the evening before.
Aunt Lydia, in London, we knew did not fail,
To send a big box ev'ry Christmas by mail.

But that kind and dear aunt, now sleeps with the dead,
For in life's early prime, her kind spirit fled;
And the friends of my youth, that made life most dear,
Have all vanished from sight this many a year.

My dear honored parents, have long gone away
But their good works remain, these ne'er will decay,
But will live through all time, and brighter will be,
As time merges on to eternity's sea.

They were kind to the poor, the needy might share
In whatever means they could possibly spare;
The outcast and stranger, a shelter could find,
Tho' cold was the season, and fierce blew the wind.

Their children were all taught old age to revere,
And the God of the heav'ns to worship and fear.
Though the Gospel restored, they never have heard,
God is righteous, and they'll not lose their reward.

Those bright Christmas pastimes could not always last,
Like the actors, they now are things of the past.
And mem'ry goes back with no sigh of regret;
Assured a bright future remains for us yet.

TO A TULIP.

SEEN IN THE GARDEN IN FEBRUARY.

Hardy flower, thou hast lifted thy head,
Above thy drear, snow-girt wintry bed,
Of all the sweet spring flowers, thou art first
To break through the garden's cold icy crust.

Fearless flower! thou hast now ventured forth,
Though the wind still comes from the biting north.
Alone thou art braving its piercing chill,
While thy sisters around thee are slumb'ring still.

Beautiful flower! glad herald of spring,
As the dove to the Ark, a promise you bring,
While spring, like the olive-branch fresh and green,
Through chill winter's lingering storms is seen.

Thou wert true to thy coming, faithful flower,
And faltered'st not though the storm clouds lower;
In thy cold prison, felt the sun's warm breath,
And hast risen again from thy seeming death.

Not dead, for in all nature's mighty range
Death is unknown; it is life, growth, and change

Harmoniously keeping creation's laws,
In obedience to a great first cause.

The humblest flower that springs from the sod,
Reveals to the eye the finger of God,
And speaks to the heart in its silence, more
Than the whirlwind's rush, or the thunder's roar.

WOMAN'S MISSION.

I never wished to be a queen,
    To wear the robes of state,
Or have my name enrolled among
    The famous or the great.

I never cared for "woman's rights,"
    Nor ever had a fear,
But that if woman sought, she'd find
    Her own, her proper sphere.

I know that woman's mission's great,
    Yet comprehends the small,
The tiny, trifling things of life,
    Important to us all.

In this, true woman finds her sphere,
    Her happiness complete,
In loving. helping, blessing all
    With whom she chance to meet.

What need for her of Congress' halls,
    Or legislative cares,
The promptings of her woman's soul,
    Is all the law she hears.

The law of love implanted there,
    By our great Parent's hand,
If not perverted, safely guides,
    Woman in every land.

I wish I had the power to write,
    Woman to vindicate,
To tell her true nobility,
    E'en in this fallen state.

I never wished for wealth or fame,
    For I have understood,
How poor and valueless are these,
    Compared with being good.

"ANOTHER OUTRAGE."

"PRESIDENT BRIGHAM YOUNG IMPRISONED IN THE PENITENTIARY."

'Tis hard to keep back the tear from the eye,
Or the blush that crimsons the cheek,
Check the angry thoughts that rise in the breast,
Or to forbid the tongue to speak:

To repress all the ire and bitter scorn,
That would force from the lips a smile,
To think that on earth a judge could be found,
So corrupt, malignant and vile.

'Twere as easy to stand by ocean's side,
And keep back the waves from the shore,
Still the tumult of the billows that toss,
When the storms in their fury roar.

To patiently wait, while an unjust judge
(Backed by minions as base as he)
Regardless of law, oppresses the just,
And then lets the wicked go free.

If saints can endure an outrage like this,
In their own beloved mountain home,
Then Utah can boast of heroes more brave,
Than those of old Sparta or Rome.

A TRUE STORY.

An Elder was preaching the Gospel in Wales,
   Without either purse or scrip,
And it happened sometimes that he had to feel
   Hunger's keen, unwelcome grip.

One day—'twas past noon—he was trav'ling along,
   Quite uncertain where to dine,
He was weary and faint, but his faith was strong,
   Nor did he feel to repine.

His heart raised in prayer, still onward he went,
   'Till a house appeared to view,
With signs of much comfort and plenty around,
   And smithy attached thereto.

Now, a blacksmith's shop is a place of resort,
   And hither he bent his way,
Very shortly a listening group had met,
   To hear what he had to say.

With truth's own eloquence, the Elder then spoke,
   And the simple story told,
That God, in these great Latter-days had restored,
   The Gospel, as 'twas of old.

He was preaching repentance, baptism for sin,
   When in came the blacksmith's wife,
Full of anger toward this servant of God,
   Like some spirit bent on strife.

Very wisely our Elder kept back the ire,
   'Twas impossible not to feel,
'Till the blacksmith's wife had expended her words
   As well as anger and zeal.

"Now madam," the Elder said, "I would enquire
   "To what sect you may belong?"

"I am a Baptist, sir, and firmly believe
  "All other religions wrong."

"You do not believe in the Testament, then?"
"Why, yes, most truly I do."
"It seems rather strange, but allow me to ask
  "If you keep it precepts too?

"You called me your enemy only just now,
  "I'm very hungry indeed,
"Therefore if thine enemy hunger, feed him,
  "Is the way my Bible reads."

A deafening shout broke from the gathered throng,
  And loudly they cheer and clap,
"There now, woman," the blacksmith laughingly said,
  "You're surely caught in a trap."

My story is told, for the sequel soon proved,
  That Philip Sykes was winner,
Without even a murmur, she sat him down
  To a substantial dinner.

CO-OPERATION.

A SONG.— *Welsh Air, Glan "Meddwdod Mwyn.*

Joy! joy! to the righteous, the good time has come,
The Latter-day Saints are uniting in one,
The Priesthood in wisdom all things will control,
And the sceptre of Jesus in peace shall bear rule.

Chorus.—Hallelujah! Hallelujah! we will not refrain,
But with the redeemed take up the glad strain,
That Jesus is coming in glory to reign.

'Tis co-operation will make us all one,
And perfect the work that in Zion's begun,
And happy are those who will join heart and hand,
To aid this great cause throughout Zion's blest land.
         Chorus.

We'll not shrink from duty when called to fulfill,
But gladly obey with our mind, might and will,
The voice of the Priesthood to us is the word,
Of Him, whom we honor, our Father and God.
         Chorus.

We are a people sought out from all climes
To help on God's work in these Latter-day times,
And never shall effort or energy cease,
'Till the Kingdom of Christ is established in peace.
         Chorus.

We've looked for the time when we shall be one,
When God's will on earth, as in heaven is done,
And the beauty of Zion, the nations shall see,
And known for their union, her people shall be.
         Chorus.

Then let us rejoice, for the good time has come,
The faithful in Zion are joining in one.
The Priesthood in wisdom, all things will control
And the sceptre of Jesus in peace shall bear rule.
         Chorus.

TO BISHOP ALBERT K. THURBER

When leaving Spanish Fork.

My dear old friend, long tried and true,
I cannot say good bye to you,
Religion's and affection's bond,
Have formed a chord of friendship fond,
And it would seem like friendship's knell
To speak that hated word—farewell.

Friends and associations, bind
You to the scenes you leave behind;
Yet, in the course of Providence
Other duties have called you hence;
Another field, a wider sphere,
Now call you from your duties here.

May you be blest where'er you go,
And prospered in whate'er you do,
Whether in teaching gospel light
To the degraded Lamanite,
In building up the saints of God,
Or preaching righteousness abroad.

Tho' here our roads may seem to part,
Faith whispers, we are one in heart,
And Hope will point with finger bright,
To happier scenes beyond our sight;
Tho' now the parting gives us pain,
Ere long we hope to meet again.

Oh, may God's blessing rest on all
Your wives, and children, great and small,
And sweet contentment ever rest
Within your home, a welcome guest,
And may we all live good and true,
Keeping life's noblest end in view.

ODE TO INDEPENDENCE DAY.

All hail to the day, when America broke
Asunder the power of dread tyranny's yoke,
And declared her intention, thenceforth to be
Independent, self governed, united and free.
All honor ! the spirit of freedom that gave
Str ngth to her people, opposition to brave,
And of all freedom's children, none more than these,
Can prize the choice blessings this day guarantees ;
But more than a century has passed since then,
And we ask with regret, where now are those men,
Whose noble intelligence, governed by right,
A people before trampled under by might ?
There were representatives then, gold could not bribe;
Who were willing all wisdom to God to ascribe,
While the statutes and laws by Congress then given,
Were first framed and sent from the councils of Heaven.
'Tis pleasing indeed, to revert back and see,
That then, in God's sight, all were equal and free ;
No paid politician dare put in a clause
To prevent any creed from keeping God's laws.
Land of my choice ! thy constitution provides
That each by the dictates of conscience decides,
And if those who make laws should swerve from the
    right,
The judge of the world will arise in His might.
Oh, my country ! now has thy proud eagle flown,
And justice, and truth have both left their throne,
While oppression and power with arrogant tread,
March over the grave of thy greatness long dead.
Else how could the blood of our martyrs have flown
When the Gospel of Christ was by Joseph made
    known ?
Its followers pleaded again and again,
For the right to serve God, but pleaded in vain ;
On Freedom's sod, persecuted and driven

From houses and lands, for which they had striven,
'Till on Mexican soil they found an abode
Where they, unmolested, could worship their God.
By patient endurance, vast wastes they reclaim,
Adding lustre and wealth to America's name;
Tho' pilgrims in exile, the home tie was dear,
And they loyally raised the Stars and Stripes here;
Through trials unheard of they've ever been true
To the flag of their country: the Red, White and Blue;
But now, 'neath that banner's broad sheltering fold,
Sad tales of oppression and wrong might be told.
Persecution's red hand is over them still,
In the form of a " Poland " or "Luttrell bill,"
Curtailing their rights, by subverting the law,
Ever seeking to find some possible flaw,
As excuse to remove all vestige of power,
Then leave them like sheep, for the wolves to devour.
But wisdom from Heaven is still given to guide
The Latter-day Saints, in whatever betide.
Though foes may be cunning, and join hand to hand,
The Saints will yet grow and inherit the land;
And if, through corruption, oppression and lust,
Columbia's glory is laid low in the dust,
Then will Utah, her country's honor sustain
And the flag of our Union, unsullied remain.

OUR NATIVE FLOWERS.

The favored flowers of other lands
    Have claimed the poet's powers;
But let our harp be tuned in praise
    Of Utah's native flowers.

We've culled them from the hilly slopes,
    From canyon's rugged side,

From low and mossy river banks,
    And from the benches wide.

We've placed them in our garden plot,
    And, growing side by side,
Their fragrance and their beauty are
    Our pleasure and our pride.

We've brought choice flowers from other climes
    And placed them near these gems,
Their mingled lustre far exceeds
    The costliest diadems.

The flowers thus brought from distant lands,
    Suggest the thought so sweet,
God's chosen ones, though scattered now,
    Together here may meet.

And like the flowers, their varied gifts,
    Improve this sacred soil,
Making the wilderness to bloom,
    Repaying care and toil.

Father, we thank thee for the flowers
    Thou hast so freely given,
And may our constant effort be
    To make this earth a heaven.

TO THE RELIEF SOCIETY OF SPANISH FORK.

Written in answer to an invitation to a Social Reunion of the Society.

Dear sisters, though most anxious, to your dance I cannot come,
For, still a prisoner I'm held within my bed at home,

What pleasure it would give me to meet with you all
    again,
To leave my bed once more, and the weary sick'ning
    pain!
But, my sisters, I am thankful, altho' the body's
    weak,
My spirit's strong and happier, than pen or tongue
    can speak.
And tho', to meet you in the dance, would give me
    much delight,
I know it is impossible, and this is why I write.
Like you, dear sisters, I enjoy the work we have to
    do,
With you, I want to labor, and to help God's King-
    dom too.
To show my gratitude to Him who called me by
    His grace,
Yet feel as if this life's too short to show forth all
    His praise.
Each one of us who knows the gospel in its truth and
    power,
And realize the blessing, which its fulness can re-
    store,
Will feel how small is the amount each one alone
    can do.
Also the need there is for love, and perfect union
    too.
The mission which we have, is a great and glorious
    one,
And num'rous blessings will accrue, if well and
    nobly done.
'Tis good that to His *daughters*, God has given
    work to do,
That not alone His *sons* must toil to bear His King-
    dom through.
To us belongs the duty, to relieve the woes we see:
Even minist'ring angels, we always ought to be.

Like good Samaritans, on hand with precious oil and
 wine,
To make the sufferers hearts we meet, with joy and
 gladness shine.
We may not see at present all the good our labors do,
But with the blessings of the Lord the harvest time
 will show,
Only let us be one in heart, and one in faith and love,
For by this test the Savior said, our love to Him we
 prove.
Evil will try to work its way, and all the good de-
 stroy,
And varied are the arts and wiles, its agents will
 employ;
But all the powers thus brought to bear by Satan and
 by sin,
Will not suffice, unless there's confederacy within.
I didn't think to write so much, but my pen was
 loth to stop,
And with reluctance even now, this pleasing subject
 drop,
So praying for God's peace to rest on every one of
 you,
With sisterly affection, bid you all a kind adieu.

COMMENT ON ACTS, 3rd CHAP. 6th VERSE.

Then Peter said, gold and silver have I none; but such as I have give I thee.

A Pontiff of Rome, by his full coffers stood,
And gazed on the treasure with which they o'er-
 flowed,
His holiness said to a priest at his side,
"That the church now is rich cannot be denied,
" 'Twas not thus in the days of Peter and John,
"Then, those Christians, of silver and gold had
 none."

The priest replied, "If wealth is measured by gold,
"The church is richer than 'twas in days of old,
"But though of our greatness and riches we talk,
"We cannot as then, bid the lame man to walk,
"And unless her wealth can this lost gift restore,
"The church, with all her silver and gold is poor."

UTAH.

A Song.—Tune—Hazel Dell.

Written for, and sung at the County Celebration of the 24th anniversary of the entrance of the Pioneers into Salt Lake Valley,—held in the Provo Woolen Factory.

We celebrate our Utah's birth,
    Glad let our songs arise
To Him whose care has guarded her,
    From danger and surprise.

Chorus—Oh! Utah hath been guarded well,
    From every danger kept,
For the eye that watched and cared for her,
    Has never, never slept.

Small, very small was Utah, then,
    And watched by many a foe,
Yet though but weak, she held the germ
    Of power and greatness too.—*Chorus*.

But soon the nation jealous grew,
    Of Utah's rising star;
And tried in vain their bolts to hurl,
    At Utah from afar.—*Chorus*.

And why has Utah thus been blest?
    Why has she favor found?
When mighty kingdoms shake and bend,
    And crumble to the ground.—*Chorus*.

Because the Lord of all the earth,
  In Utah set His throne,
And hence as ruler of the world,
  Will have His laws made known.—*Chorus.*

A living Prophet in our midst,
  Reveals God's wondrous plan,
To bless, to save, and to exalt,
  His fallen creature—man.—*Chorus.*

And hither will the honest flee,
  Ere the great judgments fall,
For every people, kindred, tongue,
  The voice of God will call.—*Chorus.*

And to that band of fearless men,
  Our noble Pioneers,
Belongs the meed of song and praise,
  Through all succeeding years.—*Chorus.*

TO MRS. ————.

ON HEARING OF HER PROTRACTED ILLNESS.

Dear suff'ring one, do not despair,
  Or think your fate is hard,
Altho' of health, great precious boon,
  Awhile you are debarred.
Think, sister dear, of all the good,
  That daily crowns your lot,
Tho' now you feel the chast'ning rod,
  Bear it and murmur not.

Think not our Father's ear is deaf,
  He hears the feeblest call,
Remember, that without His ken,
  Not e'en a sparrow falls.

Soon this dark cloud will roll away,
    And thou its lining see,
And own it was a loving hand
    That has afflicted thee.

To test thy faith and make it grow,
    Stronger and brighter, till
Each thought and purpose of thy heart,
    Blend in thy Father's will.
Believe the promises that God
    Through His own servants give,
And never doubt His power thro' them
    To bid you rise and live.

Sweet sister, as I pen the lines,
    Varied emotions well,
As, from the past I lift the veil,
    My own glad tale to tell.
Four years I lay upon my bed,
    Saw seasons come and go,
Alas! to me no change they brought,
    I still lay weak and low.

But after hope almost had fled,
    And human skill proved vain,
The Lord displayed His mighty power,
    And raised me up again.
Two of his faithful servants laid
    Their hands upon my head,
And humbly, but with mighty power,
    Spoke in their Master's stead.

The blessing sought so long had come,
    'Twas felt in every vein;
Health then returned, with all its joys,
    And pleasures in its train.
You will not wonder that my pen
    And heart should join in praise

Of Israel's God, who has restored
The Gospel in our days.

I feel, that should I hold my peace
The very stones may well
Rebuke my silence, and repeat
The words I ought to tell.
Sister, I pray that you may soon,
Health's priceless blessing know,
And join with me in praising Him,
From whom all blessings flow.

THE TWO DEACONS.

Let not the sun go down upon your wrath. Eph. 4th-36.

Two Deacons had quarrelled, but neither had felt,
To retract the harsh words, which either had dealt.
So all through that day they both stayed in their home,
Each hoping and wishing the other would come.

They were Christians, and knew that their Master had said,
Forgive, ere the sun shall have gone to his bed.
Yet often, and often, all through that long day,
Each looked at the sun as he traveled his way.

As Delf was the younger, Ward thought it was fit,
That he of the twain, should be first to submit;
"Deacon Ward is the elder," thought Deacon Delf,
"'Twere better he set the example himself."

Perturbed and unhappy, Ward paced the floor,
Each moment the sun sank lower and lower,
And he mentally said, "If I were to blame,
"I'm sure I'd be first to acknowledge the same."

Delf, from his window, saw the sun descend low,
But his heart was melted and penitent now;
"How foolish I have been," he said with a groan,
"But now for my error, I'll quickly atone."

The vict'ry was gained, he had conquered himself,
And rich in humility, was Deacon Delf,
A few moments more he was out in the road,
Approaching the house of his friend Deacon Ward,

He knew his friend's window, 'twas facing the west,
The glorious sun was just sinking to rest,
He tapped on the pane, Deacon Ward lost his frown,
"Forgive me, my brother, the sun's almost down."

Out rushed brother Ward, "You have conquered," he said,
All pride and resentment that moment had fled,
They shook hands, embraced, and were oft heard to say
They never forgot the events of that day.

A FRAGMENT.

We have waited long for spring time,
But it is come at last,
The drifting snow and biting cold
Are over now and past.
The frost and snow had bound the earth,
With fetters strong and deep;
But oh! 'tis just awaking from
Its long, long winter's sleep.
Magician's art, or magic wand
Could ne'er exert the power,
The sun's warm rays can exercise
O'er beast and bird, and flower,

It animates the insect world
Awaking them to glee,
It reacheth every living thing
And blesses all we see.

PROVO WOOLEN FACTORY.

Written in Autumn.

The leaves must all sere, and fall from the trees,
   Their mission is now to prepare,
A couch of rest on the bosom of earth,
   For the sleep of the waning year;
The chill winds may howl as they sweep along,
   With a loud and fierce warning blast,
But the sound does not fill our hearts with dread,
   As 'twas wont in years that are past.
     For often in the days of yore,
     Winter met us in clothing poor.

Now, if from those almost forgotten years,
   We call memories from their tomb,
'Tis but to enhance the gladness we feel,
   For the better days that have come.
It forces a smile, as we recollect,
   That we used to feel so secure,
If a few pounds of wool to make into cloth,
   For winter we could but procure;
     Now that the toil and care are o'er,
     We pray such times may come no more.

Just think of the lectures our children had,
   If perchance their clothing they tore,
Knowing full well, that if these were all gone,
   The trouble 'twould be to get more;
Yet they always were torn, no one knew how,

The little ones were not to blame,
They did not then wear our good Provo cloth,
  Or it would not have been the same.
    To some, this may a trifle seem,
    'Tis worth an abler pen, I deem.

Big boys with their elbows and knees all out,
  Never did look fit to be seen,
Though their mothers would stitch and patch all day,
  'Twas the *shoddy* at fault, I ween.
Our husbands and sons to the canyons went,
  Enduring the sharp biting cold,
Of the keen mountain air they had to meet,
  In clothes that were scanty and old;
    Thanks to the Factory, old and young,
    Now dress in clothes both warm and strong.

There might be imported clothes in the stores,
  But their price was fearfully high,
And Utah's productions then were not cash,
  So it was little we could buy;
Now, a load of wood will purchase a suit
  That will stand the racket and tear,
Or a nice warm shawl, or waterproof dress,
  For a wife or daughter to wear.
    There's few in this country I guess,
    The Provo Factory does not bless.

"What a blessing the Provo Factory is,"
  We oft hear from many a tongue,
And heartfelt's the prayer that to heaven ascends,
  For our President Brigham Young,
Whose unceasing care for the people's good,
  Had led him this plan to devise,
Unheeding obstacles few could surmount,
  Completed this great enterprise.
    Co-workers with him, must ne'er be forgot,
    Are the names of Bishops Smoot, Sheets, and Scott.

And now that the scales have dropped, we can see
    What we've been too slow to perceive,
The wonderful good which the co-op plan,
    In a land like this can achieve;
And all who desire our Utah's true weal,
    Hope soon the "good time," they will see,
When the people in these mountains become,
    Self-sustaining, united and free;
    And the United Order, wisely given,
    Is practiced on earth as 'tis in heaven.

INVOCATION.

While I was musing, the fire burned.—Psalm 39th—3

Sweet spirit of song! thou hast left me awhile,
And I pine for thy bright warm genial smile,
Without thee, time drags over life's weary track,
Dear spirit of song! let me welcome thee back.
Hast thou, like the song birds, sought sunnier climes?
To bask in the fragrance of myrtles and limes?
Or, like the sweet flowers, felt the frost-king's breath?
And bowed to the power of the grim tyrant—death?
Come back! for I much need thy glad presence now
That the soft summer breezes no longer blow,
No more now the rill's gentle murmur is heard,
Nor the air by soft insect music is stirred.
Come again, for I know thy presence can cheer,
E'en the wintry landscape, though gloomy and drear.
Cause the sullen mountains, a language to speak,
Though wrapt in their snow mantle, silent and bleak.
From infancy's days, thou hast oft filled my breast,
With thoughts either uttered or unexpressed.
Oft my only companion in childhood's hours,
I saw thy loved face in the sweet wild flowers;
Heard thy voice in the notes of the lark's blithe lays,

As he mounted on high his Maker to praise.
Till I caught the refrain, and, happy as he,
Thanked God, who had made such a bright world for me.
Thy presence was near in the days of my youth,
When 'mong nature's works I was searching for truth;
And feeling its chaos, my sad spirit cried
To my Father in heaven through darkness to guide.
* * * * * * * *
Inspiration! thy light on the Bible shone,
As I read how God, in past ages made known
His great mind and will from the heavens to man,
And I learned of redemption's wonderful plan.
From its pages I read that Prophets of old,
The Latter-day work, and its greatness foretold;
That the Lord would again the Gospel restore
To the earth, to be taken away no more.
The prophecies told of a kingdom and power,
Before which the kingdoms of earth should cower;
That Messiah would come to this world again
And as king on His throne forever would reign.
Inspiration! thy loved voice alone can tell,
The rapture that over my glad spirit fell
When I knew, again Jehovah had spoken,
The silence of ages at length was broken.
Let the heavens be glad, and the earth rejoice,
That again we can hear a true Prophet's voice;
Thus making God's will to His people more plain,
That they may prepare for His coming and reign.

"I WAS SICK AND YE VISITED ME."

Inscribed with much affection to Mrs. Marian R. Pratt.

Sister, your words of tenderness,
    Had power to soothe my pain,
As, on my fevered suffering head,
    They fell like gentle rain.

And even as the genial shower,
    Is to the thirsty earth,
So, sympathy and love to me,
    Are things of priceless worth.

My heart has long been weaned from things
    That many prize the most;
For, while but young, I learned the joys
    Of earth, would turn to dust.

But when the Gospel's heavenly light,
    First shone upon my way,
The spirit told of joys so pure,
    They never could decay.

And steadily truth's lustre has
    Reflected on my path,
Enough to help me cheerfully bear
    Affliction on this earth.

My life is very sweet to me,
    Great joy my spirit feels
As God in these the Latter-days,
    His wondrous plan reveals.

I've read and treasured up the words
    God's ancient prophets said,
And now His living prophet's words,
    Are more than daily bread.

But oh! it does sometimes seem hard
   To suffer day by day,
And know my time for usefulness
   Is fleeing fast away.

And this is why I'm writing now,
   'Tis all that I can do,
Though gladly would I be employed
   In active life like you.

'Tis sweet to toil from day to day,
   And know we're doing good,
By lessening the ills we meet,
   Upon life's rugged road.

Your kindness to the suffering ones,
   Your future joy will be,
Anon you'll hear your Saviour say:
   "Ye did it unto Me."

Sister, you cannot realize
   How good your visit's been;
Welcome, as on some desert bare,
   An oasis is seen.

Your honored husband's visit too
   Will be remembered long,
His words of counsel seemed to cheer
   And make my spirit strong.

He blessed me in our Father's name,
   Gently the words were given,
My lowly room then was to me
   The very gate of heaven.

But seldom has our little home,
   Held men so truly great,
Who've done so much to raise mankind
   Above their fallen state.

It seems to me this earth of ours,
  Has few such men as he,
And greatly blessed are those who share
  In his society.

Accept the heartfelt gratitude,
  My pen would fain convey,
But wish indeed, that heart and pen,
  Could worthier tribute pay.

JUBILEE HYMN.

In honor of the Seventy-fourth Anniversary of

PRESIDENT BRIGHAM YOUNG'S BIRTHDAY.

Written for, and sung at the Utah County Sunday School Jubilee, held at American Fork, June 1st, 1875.

Tune—"Crown Him." Charm, page 4.

Sing a grateful song of praise,
  To our God who reigns above,
Joyful let our voices raise,
  For His watchful care and love.

Chorus.—Praise, oh, praise the King of glory,
  Ye who know the Gospel story,
And its holy light can see,
  Keep this gladsome jubilee.

Let the children's voices swell,
  With the glad and happy strain,
Till each mountain, plain and dell,
  Echo back the sweet refrain.

JUBILEE HYMN.

Chorus.—Praise, O, praise the King of heaven,
 That he has a prophet given,
 And has spared his life to see,
 This glad birthday jubilee.

 Not for empty pomp and show,
  Not to own a tyrant's sway,
 But affection, pure and true,
  Prompts the tribute that we pay.
Chorus.—Praise, O, praise the King of heaven, etc.

 Bring not laurels that will fade
  Quickly as the world's renown,
 For his life-long deeds have made
  For him, an immortal crown.
Chorus.—Praise, O, praise, etc.

 Spare our Prophet, Lord, we pray,
  Long the saints of God to lead,
 Make us willing to obey,
  And the words of life to heed.
Chorus.—Praise, O, praise, etc.

 Shield him ever with Thine arm,
  Till his mission here is done,
 Crown him with the victor's palm,
  In the Kingdom of Thy son.

Chorus.—Crown him, crown him, King of heaven,
 Crown the Prophet Thou hast given;
 Then, with Israel's millions, free,
 Keep eternal Jubilee.

AUTUMN.

A master hand has been at work,
    With rare artistic skill,
And wrought a change on nature's face,
    O'er valley, plain and hill.

Where late adown the mountain sides,
    Naught met the eye but green,
Now, beauteous as the rainbow hues
    The autumn tints are seen.

The orchard, bright with ripening fruit,
    That 'mid the branches gleam,
Show that no grudging hand hath dealt,
    The gifts with which they teem.

We ask, what wondrous magic art,
    What great magician's wand,
So quickly, silently hath brought
    This change on every hand?

Nature, munificent and grand,
    Thine is the mighty power,
And, seeing through it, nature's God,
    We worship and adore.

And wonder at the lavish wealth,
    In such profusion spread,
To gratify the eye and taste,
    Besides "our daily bread."

And of thy gifts, kind parent, this
    Is not among the least,
That through these valleys, Thou hast giv'n
    Enough for man and beast.

The smiling plenty all around
    Is theme for joy and praise,
And cheerfully the grateful heart,
    Its willing tribute pays.

TO MY HUSBAND.

*On the Thirtieth Anniversary of our Wedding-day,
January 30th, 1881.*

Husband, dear husband, 'tis to you
　The muse directs this lay ;
Oh, may it not unwelcome prove,
　On this, our wedding day.
Just thirty years, in wedlock's chains
　We've travelled hand in hand,
Nor deemed its fetters hard to wear,
　Cemented by love's band.

Love, purest love, has ever shed
　Its halo on our path,
Making e'en trials, shared by each,
　Unlike to things of earth ;
Its power has enhanced our joy,
　Made pleasure far more sweet,
Made sorrow and affliction seem,
　Much easier to meet.

As I review life's changing scene,
　Each part looks fair and bright ;
E'en wintry landscapes take the glow,
　Of summer's rosy light.
Again I stand within the church,
　My chosen one beside,
The words are said, I leave the place,
　A thoughtful happy bride.

Words cannot tell the quiet joy,
　Which filled my spirit then,
The hopes, that in my bosom glowed,
　Defy the power of pen.
What matter if the clouds have low'red,
　Suppose the rain has dimmed,

They could not long obscure a path,
    With purest diamonds gemmed.

Each year has brought its quota fair
    Of what we prize the most,
For simple have our wishes been,
    And firm has been our trust;
True to each other, and our God,
    Casting on Him our care,
Life's storms may beat, but cannot shake,
    Our anchor, hope and prayer.

Thus, from the rainbow of the past,
    The present takes its hue,
And, on the future, throws a light,
    Subdued and trustful too.
Though youth, and prime of life are gone,
    Who knows but its decline,
Rich in the wisdom of the past,
    With holier wealth may shine!

Our children! oh, what priceless links,
    They form in wedlock's chain,
How happy in their love, to know
    We have not lived in vain.
But husband dear, how shall I close?
    How tell of all my love?
How say to you my gratitude?
    Or how its debt remove?

Frail mortal words cannot express
    Passions that are divine,
But know the heart thou gain'dst in youth,
    Is now and ever thine;
Love's eyes must read this humble rhyme,
    Nor scorn my simple theme,
For, in its light, all things though plain,
    With life and beauty teem.

WHEN I'M HAPPY.

Shall I tell you when I'm happy?
   When life to me seems very sweet?
It is when evening shadows fall,
   And we around the fireside meet.

'Tis when the children gather home,
   From school, from labor, and from play;
When little tongues all are telling,
   What they have done or learned to-day.

When each want and wish is cared for,
   Or little sorrows put to flight,
Their childish troubles all forgot,
   And every little heart is light.

"Now tell us, Ma, some pretty tale,
   " Some Bible story that you know,
" Tell us about the mighty men,
   " Who lived a long, long time ago."

From memory's store is hunted up,
   Some story to amuse or teach,
Some useful lesson, thus is taught,
   Some truth, which thus the heart may reach.

The anxious look, the listening ear,
   The tear which from the eye will steal,
The eager questions which they ask,
   Will tell how soon a child can feel.

But little eyes will sleepy grow,
   And, like the flowers, begin to close,
Like little birds, they seek their nests,
   For little forms will need repose.

The sweet good-night, and loving kiss,
   The arms that fondly twine around,
Bring to my heart such happiness
   And joy, as nowhere else is found.

TO ELDER GEO. W WILKINS,

On his departure to England on a mission to preach the Gospel.

You're going to visit the land of my birth,
That spot, once the dearest to me on the earth,
Dear still, through the friends that behind have been left,
Still loved, as my dead, there for ages have slept.

To that now distant land, my mind often turns,
For her people, my spirit in anguish yearns,
For full well I know how her poor are oppressed,
How sad is their lot, and how sorely distressed.

You will go to the poor, the honest, the meek,
To those who for truth and for righteousness seek,
You'll preach them the Gospel, yourself love so well,
Of the freedom and peace of this land you'll tell.

'Tis a noble mission, on which you now go,
A labor the angels might envy you too;
You go in your Master's great name to declare
Salvation's glad tidings to all who will hear.

And oh! may you gain many sheaves for your hire,
And accomplish the good we all most desire,
Enjoy the good spirit, where'er you may be,
Be guarded from danger, by land and by sea.

Then farewell, dear brother, 'tis needless to say,
Please think of us sometimes, while you are away,
Though absent in body, your thoughts oft will roam
To the friends you've left in your lov'd mountain home.

As saints, we must not have a parting regret,
But friends of long standing we cannot forget,
We'll think of the good time that yet is to come,
When again in our midst we welcome you home.

PIONEER DAY.

Written July 24th. 1877.

The day should be remembered long,
    That gave our Utah birth,
And handed down to every age,
    'Mong sacred days of earth.

Oh! never may our watch fires burn
    Too low to allow a flame
Of holy joy and praise to rise
    At mention of its name.

Dear Twenty-fourth! thy morning broke,
    Where none but Indians roam;
Night closed upon a pilgrim band,
    Who for truth's sake had come.

And now within these western wilds,
    To make a home essayed,
Where they could serve the God of heaven
    And none make them afraid.

This land, so long a barren waste,
    Soon yielded to the plow,
And industry, in faith begun,
    The soil to plant and sow.

The blessings of our Father, God,
    Upon the land was shed,
That Israel's multitudes who come,
    In plenty may be fed.

The dew, the rain, and mountain streams,
    Have freely lent their aid,
And bounteous nature, at their call,
    A liberal tribute paid.

For us, the elements afford,
  Meat, honey, wine and milk,
And, in their varying change they give
  Wool, cotton, hemp and silk.

Delicious fruits our gardens grace,
  Flowers shed their sweets around,
While, in our fields the staff of life,
  The precious grains abound.

New cities, towns and hamlets rise,
  Mines open up their wealth,
And Utah's thousands now enjoy,
  Peace, liberty and health.

Forgive me, if I linger long,
  On theme I love so well,
Theme, that would take an angel's pen,
  In proper guise to tell.

How rich we are, how greatly blest!
  Around, on every hand,
We see God's watchful care and love,
  Guarding this chosen land;

Shielding from harm, or warding off
  Each often threat'ning ill,
'Till Utah, in her strength has grown,
  And lives, and prospers still.

Oh! may our Utah ever shine,
  In all that's good and fair,
And may she never cease to own
  Our Heavenly Father's care.

MUTABILITY.

'Tis a world of change; but yesterday
The flowers in the garden were bright and gay.
To-day, they droop like an army slain,
And we only view them with feelings of pain.
Some had succumbed to the early frost,
And, saving to memr'y, have long been lost,
Others more hardy, braving each storm,
Stood proudly erect in their beauty and form.
I watched o'er my pets with pride and joy,
Not dreaming alas, that the frost would destroy.
It came in the night with silent tread,
And numbered my favorites among the dead;
Heedless alike of color or age,
Destroying their beauty in every stage.
The bud just formed, the full blown flower,
Alike had to bow to its mighty power,
Fit emblem, the frost, with blighting breath
To the king of terrors, the dread monster, death.
But the thoughts that my spirit oppressed,
Soon gave place to a gladness, that filled my breast,
At thought of the time frost will not come,
When perennially the flowers will bloom.

RE-UNION OF THE Y. L. M. I. A.

Written at the request of Mrs. M. J. Morrison, President for the second anniversary of the Association, Spanish Fork, April 2nd, 1877.

With joyful hearts we've met again,
    To celebrate this day,
And to the giver of all good,
    Our best devotion pay.

We thank him that our lives are spared
   Again in peace to meet,
And interchange our thoughts and words,
   In this reunion sweet.

We praise Him for the daily good,
   His hand in mercy showers,
For special blessings granted us,
   In this dear land of ours.

So blest above all other lands,
   Since here, and here alone,
A chosen Prophet of the Lord,
   His will to us makes known.

'Tis here a temple has been reared,
   To Israel's mighty king,
Which, to the living and the dead
   Will endless blessings bring.

Oh! truly we, dear sisters, are
   Among the greatly blest,
And knowing this, we each should try
   To do our duty best.

Each of us has a mission here,
   And life is very short,
Then how important 'tis to us,
   To employ it as we ought.

To seek for wisdom from above,
   That all we hear may tend,
To fit us for the life that is,
   And that which ne'er will end.

WE ARE MARCHING ON.

Written for the Spanish Fork Sunday School, and sung at the Utah County Sunday School Jubilee, held at Payson City, July 24th, 1876.

Tune.—We're Marching On.—Charm, Page 124.

We are marching on! we are marching on!
A little Mormon band;
We seek to know and please God, too,
In this, His chosen land,
Where sin, and all its ills should cease,
And ignorance must flee
Before the might of Gospel light,
And the truth will make us free.

Chorus.—We are marching on! we are marching on!
And though the way be long,
We'll keep it bright, with faith by night,
And glad by day with song.

We are marching on! we are marching on!
A glad and happy throng,
Who love the truth, and in our youth,
Would help its cause along,
We'll show our gratitude to those
Who've taught us what is right;
And never stray from wisdom's way,
But keep it day and night.—*Chorus.*

We are marching on! we are marching on!
And call on old and young,
On every hand, in every land,
From every clime and tongue,

  To come with us our God to serve,
   And learn His mind and will,
  Where He will guide what'er betide
   With revelation still.—*Chorus.*

We are marching on! we are marching on!
  Then come with us and raise,
Your voice to swell, the song to tell.
  Of our Redeemer's praise,
Till all the pure in heart shall know
  The Gospel's power to save;
Our flag, unfurled, before the world,
  Shall never cease to wave.—*Chorus.*

TO MRS. S. M. HEYWOOD.

SALT LAKE CITY.

The waters of sorrow are troubled and deep,
  Through which I am now called to go,
While 'round me the billows dash angry and loud
  As if threatening to overflow.

Yet I shall not sink, for my feet are placed firm
  On a rock that cannot remove;
And though sorely battered, I lean on the arm
  Of One, who Almighty will prove.

It is hard sometimes, in the mists that enshroud,
  To discern a glimmer of light;
But anon, in the gloom, the small voice is heard
  "Struggle on and all will be right."

And then, oh! how welcome and sweet at such times
  Is the kind encouraging word,
That friendship can offer, or love can suggest,
  And oh! with what gladness 'tis heard.

But words fail to express how grateful I feel,
  For the comfort your note contains;
It spoke to my spirit, so wounded and sore.
  And soothed the dull wearying pains.

Perhaps, when the thick cloud of trouble rolls off,
  And the sun is shining again,
I yet may emerge from the darkness and gloom,
  And indulge in a happier vein.

Till then, dearest sister, accept my warm thanks,
  'Tis all I can offer to you;
That the choicest blessings may rest on you all,
  Is the prayer of yours,—adieu.

A PLEA FOR THE RELIEF SOCIETY.

Written at the request of Mrs. Rhoda Snell, first President of the Relief Society of Spanish Fork and read at the celebration of the 24th of July, 1867.

Gather up the fragments, that nothing be lost. John, Chap. VI. ver. 12.

Let us gather up the fragments,
  That nothing may be lost,
And never mind how trifling, or
  How small may be their cost.

Economy is heaven's law,
  Let us observe and see;
A tiny drop, a single grain,
  Each of some use can be.

Union is strength, and when we meet
  And in one cause unite,
Much may be done to help and bless,
  And make the burden light.

We bring our little bits of cloth,
    Our bunch of wool or thread ;
And busy fingers work awhile;
    And soon a quilt is made.

We give our mite the poor to help,
    Their pressing wants relieve,
But do we realize how much,
    We each from God receive?

On this glad day, when through these vales,
    The saints with joy have met,
Can we while pleasure thrills the heart,
    The absent ones forget?

Our people now in distant lands,
    Would glad these blessings share,
And from them oft, for help from us,
    Ascends the fervent prayer.

Oppressed with poverty, they sigh,
    While sin and crime abound ;
And evils now unknown to us,
    Encompass them around.

By us a Prophet's voice is heard,
    Our eyes can see his face,
Would they not prize above all joys,
    In Zion's land a place?

Perhaps the little we have done,
    Is registered on high,
And, when the books at last are read
    Will not unnoticed lie.

But do we each give all we can
    When any call is made?
Or is our first desire to know
    How little can be paid?

Does it sometimes seem hard to part
    With what we earn so dear ?
As Saints of God we ought to live
    Above all selfish fear.

'Tis faith alone, can understand
    The charge so wisely given,
(Though some may fear to run the risk,)
    "Lay treasures up in Heaven."

A PRAYER.

Written Jan 8th, 1872, on the occasion of President Brigham Young being arraigned before Chief Justice James B. McKean on a charge of murder.

Low at thy feet, oh, Lord of Hosts we bow,
And ask Thee to regard our Prophet now ;
Save him, our Father, from those wicked men,
As Thou didst Daniel, in the lion's den.

Thousands of Israel, on their bended knee,
With hearts sincere are looking up to Thee,
Praying, that in this dark and threat'ning hour,
Thou wouldst now make known Thy mighty power.

Hush Thou the tumult in Thy people's breast,
For now they feel how sorely they're oppressed ;
He, whom we love, our dearest earthly friend,
Is made a pris'ner by a human fiend.

The man renowned for deeds of noble worth,
Than whom, no purer dwells on Thy broad earth,
Accused of crimes at which the soul revolts.
Before a "ring" of lying sensual dolts.

To-day, Thy servant Brigham meets his foes,
On charges, every child in Utah knows
Are false and foul, as those from whom they come;
Thus innocence from guilt must hear its doom.

And will Columbia, proud nation, stain
Its honor with a blot that will remain?
And can her rulers now look on and see
This outrage on their boasted liberty?

O, Lord, arise! and let the nation see,
That this, its controversy, is with Thee,
Thy Saints, strive only to obey Thy laws,
Fulfil their duties, and maintain Thy cause.

TO MRS. MARY ANN JONES.

Smithfield, Cache Co.

My ever dear friend, I only can say
  In excuse for my seeming neglect,
That I did not know you cared for my rhymes,
  Or a word from my pen would expect.

Forgive me this time, in future I'll try
  And not give you just cause to complain,
I prize the gift that on me is bestowed,
  And desire to give pleasure, not pain.

Words fail to tell the delight it has been,
  Through long years of suffering and pain,
To rise, like the lark, in its morning song,
  And find vent in the jubilant strain.

'Tis best to extract all the sweet we can,
  Nor repine if life's journey is rough,
'Tis wisdom to look on the brightest side,
  We are sure to have darkness enough.

We each have our own peculiar ills,
  While each heart its own bitterness knows,
'Till it seems as if we surely must sink,
  'Neath the weight of our manifold woes.

Then out from the depths of sorrow and pain,
  Comes the earnest, and powerful prayer;
And we cast our trouble and care on One,
  Who is able and willing to bear.

Oh! can we not see that Infinite love,
  Directs all our affairs here below,
Let us trust that love, while here we remain,
  'Till again to God's presence we go.

BEAUTIFUL MOUNTAIN HOME.

Written for the Spanish Fork Sunday School.

Tune—Beautiful Home Above. American Tune Book, page 351.

Oh! how my spirit loveth thee,
  Beautiful mountain home,
Here I can dwell from bondage free,
  Beautiful mountain home.
Within these happy vales of light,
Adorned with virtues pure and bright,
I'll dwell with those who do what's right,
  In my mountain home.

Chorus—Beautiful mountain home!
  Beautiful mountain home!
O, help me Lord, to do Thy will,
  In my beautiful mountain home.

Thy peace I seek, and daily pray,
  Beautiful mountain home;

For strength to walk the narrow way,
  Beautiful mountain home;
My mind will seek from learning's lore,
What those have taught who went before,
And gain what's for the good in store,
  In my beautiful home.—*Chorus.*

Thy glorious future now I see,
  Beautiful mountain home;
The city where the just shall be,
  Beautiful mountain home.
And I will keep my longing eyes
Intently fixed upon the prize,
'Till Zion in her beauty rise,
  My happy, happy home.

Chorus—Beautiful mountain home!
Beautiful mountain home!
O, help me Lord to do Thy will,
In my happy, happy home.

TO MRS. MARY ISAACS.

*On the Thirty-Ninth Anniversary of her Birthday,
April 25th, 1880.*

Dear friend, accept the tribute due,
Which now my pen would offer you,
Accept the wish and heartfelt prayer,
That God may make your life His care,
And spare you yet, many a year,
  To those to whom you are most dear.

In honoring Polygamy,
The Lord will bless and honor thee;
Will prosper thee forever more,

Alike in basket and in store;
Much of His goodness you will see,
In this glad year of Jubilee.

Sustain thy husband, help him, too,
Since, on a mission called to go,
Do thou thy best to cheer him up,
Nor add one drop to sorrow's cup.
Only be faithful, do not doubt
God's peace will compass you about.

I sympathize with him and you—.
And each one of his household, too,
For all will keenly feel the smart,
E'en for a little while to part;
But may each see their duty plain,
Nor ever murmur or complain.

So ,wishing you many returns of the day,
I will put my pen, ink and paper away.

•LEAD ME TO THE ROCK.

When my heart is overwhelmed, lead me to the rock that is higher than I.
Psalm 61—2 verse.

When my spirit with sorrow is overwhelmed,
  Then, from out of the depths comes the cry,
As my earthly friends leave me, lead me I pray,
  " To the rock that is higher than I."

As my children, by death, are called from my arms,
  To their Father and Mother on High;
Then, all lonely and weak, I pray to be led,
  " To the rock that is higher than I."

In affliction's dark hour, when heart and flesh fail,
  And temptations my faith sorely try,

Then, more earnest I cling, for strength and defense,
  "To the rock that is higher than I."

If prosperity sheds its light on my path,
  And kind friends, to encourage, are nigh,
In thanksgiving and praise, I ever am led,
  "To the rock that is higher than I."

When I seek at earth's cisterns, my thirst to assuage,
  And find them all broken and dry,
Then lead me I pray, for the life-giving draught,
  "To the rock that is higher than I."

Or, when persecution and trouble assail,
  And their arrows are swift hurling by,
I fear not the shafts; while for shelter I'm led
  "To the rock that is higher than I."

E'en death, the last enemy cannot destroy,
  While upon a strong arm I rely;
The Priesthood eternal is leading me on,
  "To the rock that is higher than I."

WINTER.

Stern winter has come, with its chilling breath.
Nature is touch'd by the finger of death.
The flowers that lately were blooming gay
Felt its cold breath, and have withered away.

The sweet birds of song have taken their flight,
To regions where flowers and sunshine are bright,
Insects and reptiles are hid in repose,
Far out of reach of the frost and the snows.

The picture's sad, and our spirits would droop,
Were't not that the future is cheered by hope,

Which bids us remember, that winter drear,
Must give place to spring, with pleasures so dear.

This makes us think, how our Father in Heaven,
Enjoyment in every season has giv'n,
The summer, the autumn, winter and spring,
Much good in their change to us ever bring.

JULY 24th, 1872.

The Twenty-fourth again is here,
The gladdest day of all the year,
And from our heart's deep fountains spring,
Our heartfelt thanks, to God our King.

We've watched our young and rising state,
First small, but daily growing great,
'Till now we feel an honest pride,
To be with her identified.

Twenty-five years have wonders done,
Yet Utah has but just begun;
And humbly, gratefully we say,
Thank God for what she is to-day.

From Him has come the mind and sense,
The governing power, intelligence,
And wisdom that has made our state,
Now honored 'mong the nations great.

Utah has had the uphill grade,
Through difficulties great to wade,
Yet through them all, the giant stride,
Shows how her foes were all defied.

Onward and upward, bright and clear,
From day to day, from year to year,

Yet steadily advancing on,
Pursuing right, avoiding wrong.

We ask, what will her future be
But happy, glorious and free?
Though clouds may low'r, and threaten yet,
Our Utah's sun will never set.

MUSINGS.

I often think, in my musings,
   How happy our frail lives would be,
If instead of the dark side of things,
   Their bright side, we always could see.

We've need of all the sweet sunshine
   We can get on life's gloomy way,
Oh! then let us catch ev'ry glimpse,
   Of its bright and fast fleeting ray.

In every condition of life,
   Whatever our trials below,
Thrice happy to us is the thought,
   Of "Father," to whom we may go.

Suppose, in the fog that surrounds,
   We've happened to take the wrong road,
Let's seek till we find the right gate,
   That leads to our Father's abode.

Look not wistfully to the past,
   Which can never return again,
'Tis vain to brood o'er thoughts that fill
   The present with sorrow and pain.

If childhood's days were pure and free,
   If youth had been happy and clear,

Why should its lustre be tarnished
  By the bitter regretful tear.

Should sickness spread o'er us its shade,
  Where health was accustomed to bloom,
Let's think of the land that's before,
  Where dread sickness never can come.

Should our lot be sorrow and grief,
  Repining will surely be vain,
We never have more than our share,
  Of grief's bitter measure to drain.

And often, in draining the dregs,
  Joy's sweet, purest drop we may find,
When the clouds of sorrow roll off,
  The silver lined cloud lies behind.

SONG.—DESERET.

Tune—Brattle Street—American Tune Book, page 156.

My heart is with thee, Deseret,
  Thy people are my choice,
And I will sing thy praises yet,
  With glad and joyful voice.

Chorus—Oh! Deseret, dear Deseret!
  Home of the saints, how dear;
To all whose hearts on truth are set,
  Thy beauties now appear.

I love thy mountains, Deseret,
  Their grand sublimity;
And never will my heart regret,
  Its choice, dear land of thee.—*Chorus.*

I love thy valleys, Deseret,
  All that belongs to thee

Are things on which my mind is set,
　Thou art most dear to me.—*Chorus*.

I love thy freedom, Deseret,
　My soul delights in thee;
Here light and truth, and peace have met
　In sweet simplicity.—*Chorus*.

I love thy sabbaths, Deseret,
　'Tis joy beyond degree
To hear the words of life made known
　In truth and purity.—*Chorus*.

I love thy future, Deseret,
　The eye of faith can see,
Tho' clouds may hang around thee yet,
　Endless thy joys will be.—*Chorus*.

Blest are thy people, Deseret,
　Favored of God art thou,
Thy friends shall glory in thee yet,
　Thy foes to thee shall bow.—*Chorus*.

TRUTH.

Truth stood on a pedestal,—fair and high,
Nor flinched, as the arrows of falsehood sped by,
Around him, its squibs and crackers were hurled,
Yet boldly he stood, defying the world.

Calmly he smiled at the gathering crowd,
At the great swelling words, portentious and loud,
Which falsehood's vile minions were trying to shower,
To destroy from this earth, this much dreaded power.

But their missiles were harmless, tho' aim'd at him,
They failed his beauty or brightness to dim,
Still proudly he stood, as the crestfallen throng,
With purpose defeated, moved sadly along.

WELCOME.

Written at the request of sister Mary A. McLean, President of the Primary Association of Spanish Fork, in anticipation of the visit of sisters Loui Felt, Mary A. Freeze, Clara Y. Conrad, Zina Y. Williams, Nancy Smoot, and Mary J. Johns; to attend the 2nd anniversary of the Primary Association of Spanish Fork, Oct. 23rd, 1880, and read on that occasion.

We welcome you to Spanish Fork,
   With welcome warm and true,
And most hearty is the greeting,
   We now extend to you.

'Tis very pleasant, thus to meet,
   Amid life's busy throng,
With those, who like ourselves desire,
   To help God's work along.

Who do not grudge the time and means,
   That in truth's cause is spent,
But daily strive with hearts sincere,
   And steady purpose bent,

To fill the various missions which
   To each has been assigned,
All differing, yet their end the same,
   To instruct the human mind.

Some have to guide the little feet,
   Within the narrow way,
That from the path that leads to God,
   They may not go astray.

Others the pleasing duty find,
   To teach the rising youth,
That they may in their turn become
   Champions for the truth.

The sick, the needy, and the poor
    Claim our especial care,
Our love, our sympathy and aid,
    Our blessing and our prayer.

This wondrous work of Latter-days
    Is fitted to engage,
The head, the heart, the hands and voice
    Of every sex and age.

The Gospel field is very large,
    The faithful lab'rors few;
Then is there not enough, enough,
    For all of us to do?

Each heart responds, there is enough
    Of work around us spread,
In which each faithful saint can help,
    The living and the dead.

Then let us each, to whom is given
    One talent to employ,
So wisely use, that it may be
    Our glory and our joy,

Perhaps the little we can do,
    May to our Father show,
That we appreciate the debt
    Of gratitude we owe.

We trust your little visit here
    To you and us may prove,
A happy interchange of thought
    Of friendship and of love.

That you may take back to your homes
    Some kindly thought from here,
That we may hold your memory sweet,
    Our interview most dear.

SONG—STRIVE FOR THE RIGHT.
Written for the Utah County Sunday School Jubilee.
Tune—On to the Goal. Charm, Page 70.

Strive for the truth, let's strive,
  Glory will wreath the brow,
Of those who in truth's cause,
  Make all that oppose it bow;
We'll gird our armor on,
  Keep sword and helmet bright,
And let the watchword be,
  Truth, union, freedom, right.
Chorus.—Strive for the truth, friends, strive,
  Victory will crown the brow,
Of those who in truth's cause,
  Make all that oppose it bow.

On for the prize, right on,
  Tho' 'tis o'er hostile ground,
Tho' foes are great and strong,
  And dangers thick abound;
We'll on, forever on,
  There's no such word as fail.
The Priesthood's mighty law,
  Will o'er earth as heav'n prevail.—*Chorus.*

Strive to be one, let's strive,
  To us the God of heaven,
Has in these Latter-days,
  The United Order given;
And young as well as old,
  The poor, the weak, the strong,
Can aid the impulse given,
  And roll the work along.
Chorus.—The young as well as old,
  The poor, the weak, the strong,
Can aid the impulse given,
  And roll the work along.

CONSOLATION.

Prompted when in deep sorrow on account of my daughter.

Thou troubled one, dismiss thy care,
Look to thy God by humble prayer,
Commit thy daughter to His love,
Who listens from His throne above.

Though thou hast been by care oppressed,
Cast it on Him, He'll give thee rest,
For all who come with heart sincere,
Our Father, God, will ever hear.

Your child He'll bless and always guide,
Whenever danger may betide,
Her life He will in safety keep,
For Israel's God will never sleep.

Soon thou shalt see and shalt rejoice,
And know it is the spirit's voice,
That bids thee every care resign,
And trust the hand that is divine.

Thy husband, too, shall joy in me,
And clearer shall his vision be;
Though often called to bear the rod,
He shall rejoice in me, his God.

Uphold thy husband, comfort him,
Should e'er his faith grow cold or dim,
For thou wast given him for joy,
That nothing ever can destroy.

Together from your native land,
You've gathered with my chosen band,
A work to do, a place to fill,
To honor me and do my will.

And though the darkness gather round,
'Till scarce a ray of light is found,
I'll never leave thee, nor forsake,
But to my glory, thee I'll take.

Thy children, too, thy head shall crown,
With endless glory and renown;
Then fear thee not, but ever trust,
And know thy God is wise and just.

RETURNING MISSIONARIES.

A welcome to Elders Thos. C. Martell and Thos. D. Evans—Superintendents of Sabbath School—on their return from a mission to Wales.

Welcome, brethren! glad we welcome
    You to home and friends again,
And we feel that joy at meeting,
    Compensates for parting pain.

Welcome, brethren! we have missed you
    From your home and duties here,
While you went to fill your mission
    In a distant land and sphere.

Welcome, brethren! smiling nature
    Seems to welcome you again,
With her wealth of summer beauty,
    With her fruits and flowers and grain.

Welcome, brethren! while we render,
    Grateful thanks to Him who holds
Within his hand the winds and waves,
    And for you their power controls.

Welcome, brethren ! you are welcome
    To the place you used to fill
In our sabbath school, and welcome
    To each child's affection still.

Welcome, brethren ! though forth you went
    Weeping, bearing precious seeds,
You have come with sheaves of gladness
    As the Bible's promise reads.

Welcome, brethren ! to these Valleys,
    All the good will welcome you,
May you hear the Master's plaudit.
    Well done, servants tried and true !

MEMORY OF CHILDHOOD.

"Maria" and I, were busy one day,
Clearing a lot of old rubbish away
From a nook in the brickyard, whence that morn,
The last load of bricks from that place was drawn.
Now we, happy girls, had thought of a plan,
And in childish glee to my mother ran ;
A garden we'd make and plant it with care,
And sweet little flowers soon should grow there.
My kind mother feared our pleasure to chill,
Yet hinted, the spot might be needed still.
But we were so full of our pleasant scheme,
That reason or sense must not spoil the dream ;
So we dug up the ground with care and toil,
And prepared for the flowers the nice fresh soil.
We watered and tended our garden well,
How delighted we were, no words could tell.
But alas for our joys, the kiln was burned,
And out of it soon the bricks must be turned.

One morning, the master was looking 'round,
'Twas then the trim little garden he found.
He asked the steward, "by whom was this done?"
And was told, "by the girls in innocent fun."
Mr. Sharman, who'd ever to us been kind,
To faults and follies persistently blind;
Had good cause to fear some censure just then
From his stern employer, Mr. George Fenn,
Who looked at the flowers so bright and sweet,
At the fence we'd made so pretty and neat;
Their silent appeal had well done its part,
Touched a tender chord in the proud man's heart.
As he gazed, his face wore a softer look;
At length to the steward again he spoke,
"'Tis a pity the children put them here,
"For the place we cannot possibly spare."
Then with urbanity and feeling rare,
He selected a spot with thoughtful care.
Maria and I were hid in a shed
From which we could hear whatever was said;
Just imagine our joy, 'twas past belief,
A moment before, we were bowed with grief.
We were land holders now, richer, I ween,
Than some worth thousands of acres have been;
Our new garden was large, while we were small,
Hence not equal to the task of digging it all.
But the "brick boys" helped with strong hand and arm,
And the work was done as if by a charm;
Those kind hearted boys were happy as we,
They worked and whistled in boyish glee,
Then put in a claim, we did not contest,
For a flower to put in their Sunday vest.
There early in spring bright flowers were seen,
Peeping forth from out their setting of green.
The snowdrop, crocus and proud daffodil,
With daisy, cowslip and dainty jonquill,

The pure queen of May, and famed London pride,
With blue bells and pinks, bloomed here side by
 side ;
In summer-time too, there was plenty of room,
For roses and lilies to give sweet perfume.
We planted medicinal herbs for tea,
For dolls, and kittens might get sick you see,
A school-mate was doctor, and sexton beside,
To 'tend the sick, and inter if they died,
Then, as we still had a corner to spare,
We thought 'twould be best to lay out a square ;
Soon little hillocks and stones marked each spot
Where our pets were buried, but ne'er forgot.
Those funerals, ah, me ! were *mimic* affairs,
The actors then knew no sorrow or cares,
No matter, then, what the future would be,
The present at least was happy and free;
But time has been busy, long years since then,
Those children have grown to women and men,
Each acting their part on life's busy stage
Writing their names on futurity's page.

DECEMBER 25TH.

*Written for the Young Ladies Mutual Improvement
Association.*

All Christian nations keep this day,
 To celebrate the birth
Of Jesus Christ, who came to pay
 Our ransom on this earth.

The history of his advent,
 By sacred writers told,
Who chronicled the great event,
 By prophets long foretold,

Is full of interest, and is read
    In every tongue and clime ;
Sages and poets wrote and sang,
    Upon the theme sublime.

And I would tune my humble lyre,
    And in my lowly way,
Would tell the thoughts my heart inspire
    In prospect of this day.

An angel came from heaven's throne,
    The joyful news to bring
To Bethle'm's shepherds, that "to-day
    "Is born a Saviour king."

Then suddenly a multitude
    Of holy angels came,
And in seraphic measure sang,
    Praise to our Father's name.

"Glory to God in the highest,
    And to the earth be peace,
For unto us is born the Christ,
    Whose reign will never cease."

The shepherds who these tidings heard,
    Hastened to Bethlehem,
And there the holy babe was found
    As it was told to them.

Wise men from Eastern lands afar,
    Came with an offering ;
And guided thither by a star,
    They found the infant king.

And worshipped the holy child,
    While at his feet they laid
Their gifts ; (gold, frankincense and myrrh,)
    Which mystic homage paid.

Gold signified him to be king;
  Myrrh, that he was to die;
The incense showed him to be God,
  Son of the Lord Most High.

He died a sacrifice for sin,
  And yielded up his breath,
To remove the curse of Adam's guilt
  By his vicarious death.

The Saviour's birth, his life and death,
  Were pure and free from blame,
And we, his followers, should strive
  To make our lives the same.

Methinks, dear sisters, we shall best
  Keep Christmas holiday,
If love to God and all mankind
  Within our hearts bear sway.

DEPARTING MISSIONARIES.

Written by request, for a surprise party given to five missionaries, previous to their departure to England, Scotland and Iceland.

Our brethren have been called upon, to distant lands to go,
And to those that dwell in darkness, the Gospel light to show,
To warn the people of their doom, when Babylon shall fall,
And in its sure destruction, will engulf the wicked all,
That the poor within those nations, downtrodden and oppressed

May hear and gather to this land, above all others
  blest,
That the dead may be remembered, who sleep with-
  in the grave,
That we for them may do a work which will exalt
  and save.
The elders have responded to this most important
  call,
Are willing to forsake their homes, their wives and
  children all,
To break association's ties, from friends and kindred
  part,
And to leave the land of Zion, so dear to each true
  heart.
They go with love and sympathy, accompanied by
  prayer,
That God, even Israel's God, may make their lives
  His care.
Ward off every threatened ill, either by land or sea,
And in each strait or need may then His tender
  mercy see.
Oh, may their faith in God be strong, whatever may
  betide,
And firmly trust that, day by day, He will for them
  provide.
This brings to mind a circumstance which I remem-
  ber well,
Having heard a traveling Elder, his own experience
  tell.
He was just then laboring in the Norwich Confer-
  ence,
And found himself at nightfall, without either food
  or pence,
Hungry, shelterless, cold and lone, he knew not
  where to go,
No saints lived near, to whom to turn; what now
  was he to do?

Soon thinking of "Our Father," to Heaven he raised his eyes,
Breathing meanwhile a fervent prayer, look'd upwards to the skies,
"Oh! give me sixpence, Lord, I must have sixpence," again he said ;
"Sixpence is all I ask, just to procure me food and bed."
Then looking down, with joy he saw, a silver sixpence lay,
So bright and new it might have come fresh from the mint that day.
He picked the shining treasure up, glowing with gratitude,
His wants supplied, with joy next day, his journey he pursued.

―――◆◆◆―――

A SONG OF PRAISE.

Written for the Spanish Fork Sunday School.

Tune—Just Starting out. Charm—page 58.

Come let us sing a gladsome song,
  To our Redeemer's praise,
For all the blessings we receive
  In these great Latter-days.

Chorus.—We'll come, we'll come, we'll come to Sunday-school,
We'll try, we'll try to practice every rule.

The children in these happy vales,
  Above all others blest,
Have cause to praise the Lord above,
And try to serve him best.—*Chorus.*

We thank Him for our teachers kind,
 For good instruction given,
For Gospel light, to guide us here,
 And lead us back to heaven.—*Chorus.*

Of all that dwell upon the earth,
 None are so blest and free,
And gratitude inclines our hearts,
 Our Father, God, to thee.—*Chorus.*

From every soul, like incense pure,
 Our songs of joy shall rise,
Till angels catch the glad refrain
 And bear it to the skies.—*Chorus.*

A HAPPY NEW YEAR.

Inscribed to the brothers William, Thomas, James, John, Alexander and Charles O. Robertson, and read at a social reunion given in commemoration of the twentieth anniversary of their leaving Scotland to gather to Zion, January 1st, 1870.

A happy new year to all that are here,
 And many more years to enjoy;
Health, happiness, peace, prosperity too,
 And pleasure without alloy.

New Year is a time for all to be glad,
 Who've wisely disposed of the old,
And can turn its pages over and know
 That no stain disgraces its fold.

New Year's a time to look forward with hope,
 And resolve the future shall see

Us employed to the best of our power,
  And higher our motto should be.

But to some here to-day, this New Year brings
  Recollections twenty years back;
Recalling memories of long ago,
  As they glance o'er life's beaten track.

'Tis now twenty years since last they beheld,
  The hills of old Scotia's land,
And bade adieu to the place of their birth,
  To dwell on Columbia's strand.

While gratefully now they review the past,
  And acknowledge the hand of God,
Who has given to them a name and place
  On Zion's thrice favored sod.

More truly honored are they, and their names
  On posterity's stream shall descend,
When the mighty ones of earth are forgot,
  And their line ignobly shall end.

Some sorrow may sadden their joy to think
  Of their mother, left by the way,
Whose dust reposes, as laid by her sons,
  On the heights of remote Iowa.

And who shall say how her spirit has watched
  O'er the sons she had to resign;
Or how her influence 'round them has been,
  To elevate, bless and refine?

And now we will wish, that the coming years,
  May find all the brothers still true
To the faith they hold, to the God they serve,
  And favored and prosperous too.

THINK OF THY MOTHER.

Addressed to the children of Mrs. Gwyn Morgan Lewis, who gathered to this land for the Gospel's sake, having left all her kindred.

And I will take you one of a city, and two of a family, and bring you to Zion —Jer. III.—14.

Think of thy mother, now aged, and far
    From the land that has given her birth,
Called thence by a power she could not resist,
    To dwell on this part of the earth.

Think of thy mother, for often and fond,
    She thinks of the sons she has left,
And sadly she yearns for their care and love,
    Of which she has long been bereft.

Not one son or daughter to cheer her path,
    As she treads the down hill of life,
Or help her to bear the burden or care,
    With which the journey is rife.

She is not unhappy, here she has found
    Friends who are loving and kind;
She trusts in her God, who will not forsake;
    Thus calm and serene is her mind.

Still she prays that her children, too, may see
    This marvelous Latter-day work,
That can gather from ev'ry land and unite
    In one fold, the " Christian and Turk."

This wonderful work predicted so long,
    God's kingdom set up on the earth,
He calls by His spirit, the honest of heart,
    Irrespective of country or birth.

One of a family, city or town,
  May hear the still voice and obey,
And the sacrifice they're called on to make
  God is bound by His word to repay.

I know your good mother, and love her much,
  Our hearts have felt sympathy's bond,
Like her I have left my country and kin,
  Severed ties most sacred and fond.

Through years of sickness, her visits to me
  Have been welcome as day's gladsome light,
Her words of comfort have often beguiled
  Affliction's long wearisome night.

I've learned to call her the *tenderest* name,
  And often and earnestly pray,
That her precious life may yet be prolonged,
  And death may be still far away.

ON THE BIRTH OF OUR GRANDSON,

SAMUEL HOLLINGSWORTH CORNABY.

Spanish Fork, Oct. 19, 1878.

Father, Mother, in the heaven
  Thou hast sent our sweet baby here ;
We thank thee for the treasure given
  And will prize the gift most dear.

May our little darling grow,
  Blest of Thee from day to day ;
And fill his mission here below,
  Nor ever from Thy precepts stray.

Bless his parents with the wisdom
  And the patience which they need,

That their offspring may become
    Mighty for truth in word and deed.

Baby, darling, take the welcome
    Of thy parents' loving heart,
Welcome to thy earthly home
    Weak and helpless though thou art.

Thy brother Willie, baby still,
    In his guileless joy and glee,
Hugs and kiss with right good will
    Does his best to welcome thee.

Thy uncles, aunts, and cousins join
    To bid thee kindly welcome here,
And pray that love and power divine,
    May guide thee through this world of care.

Grandparents' prayers, and wishes blend,
    That blessings of the heavens and earth,
May through life's changing scenes attend
    Their grandson Samuel Hollingsworth.

RESPONSE TO MRS. R————.

Thanks for your lines, they call me back to girl-
    hood's happy days,
Ere yet to me life's path had known, aught but the
    sun's bright rays,
When love and hope and health for me their treasures
    spread around,
When roses bloomed along my path, and ne'er a
    thorn was found.
My native land, my parents dear, sisters who loved
    so true,
And friends whose gentle tenderness I now remem-
    ber too;

My books, my studies, and old scenes, came as by
    magic spell
Of some fond vision of the past, remembered now
    so well.
I draw the contrast; tho' not sad that contrast seems
    to me,
For brighter still, and happier far, life now appears
    to be.
Thus far life's journey I have trod, with all its joys
    and care,
And through each chequered changing scene my
    anchor has been prayer.
A firm unwavering trust in God, my Father and my
    friend,
Has led me on through every stage, and will till life
    shall end.
I know that He who sought me out, when yet I knew
    Him not,
Will never leave me, nor forsake, tho' humble be my
    lot.